## Asset Management (AM)

# Retirement Plan Products and Services

February 2014

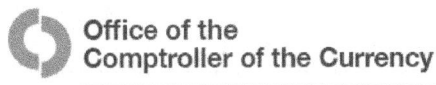

**Office of the
Comptroller of the Currency**

Washington, DC 20219

# Contents

# Introduction

The Office of the Comptroller of the Currency's (OCC) *Comptroller's Handbook* booklet, "Retirement Plan Products and Services," provides comprehensive guidance to examiners and bankers regarding retirement plan products and services offered to customers of national banks and federal savings associations (collectively, banks, except when it is necessary to distinguish between the two). This booklet explains the risks inherent in such products and services and provides a framework for managing those risks. This booklet also provides optional examination procedures, which supplement the core assessment standards in the "Large Bank Supervision" and "Community Bank Supervision" booklets of the *Comptroller's Handbook*. Examiners should use this booklet's optional examination procedures when specific products, services, or risks warrant review beyond the core assessment.

Offering retirement plan products and services exposes banks to a range of risk factors. The nature and scope of a bank's products and services determine which risks are present and what the quantity of those risks are. Given the variety of laws and regulations that apply to retirement accounts, compliance risk is inherently high. Because personal retirement assets are involved and there is frequently a fiduciary relationship between the bank and its customers, reputation risk is also a substantial factor. Given the volume of transactions associated with many retirement plan product and service relationships, operational risk is high. If a bank offers a new or complex retirement plan product or service or has an outsourcing arrangement with a domestic or foreign entity, strategic risk increases.

The Employee Retirement Income Security Act of 1974 (ERISA), its corresponding regulations found at 29 CFR Chapter XXV, and the Internal Revenue Code (IRC) are the primary sources of law governing the structure, administration, and operation of employee benefit plans. The U.S. Department of Labor (DOL), through the Employee Benefits Security Administration (EBSA), is responsible for administering and enforcing ERISA. ERISA is summarized in appendix C of this booklet. The Internal Revenue Service (IRS) is responsible for administering and enforcing the IRC. When providing products and services to retirement plans, whether or not the plans are subject to ERISA, national banks must comply with 12 CFR 9 and federal savings associations must comply with 12 CFR 150, as well as any other applicable law. OCC Bulletin 2006-24, "Interagency Agreement on ERISA Referrals: Information Sharing Between the FFIEC Agencies and the DOL," reflects the federal banking agencies' longstanding commitment to refer possible significant violations of ERISA to the DOL.

Employee benefit plans are a vital part of workers' total compensation and help employers attract and retain personnel. ERISA divides the term "employee benefit plans" into two general groups:

- Employee pension benefit plans
- Employee welfare benefit plans

Employee pension benefit plans can be qualified or nonqualified. Qualified plans "qualify" for special tax treatment under the IRC. Qualified plans can be further broken down into two categories: defined benefit plans and defined contribution plans. Nonqualified employee pension benefit plans defer compensation and provide benefits payable at retirement or termination of employment but do not qualify for favorable tax treatment. Generally, nonqualified employee pension benefit plans include executive or incentive compensation arrangements. Employee welfare benefit plans provide such benefits as medical, dental, life, and disability insurance coverage. While the focus of this booklet is on qualified employee pension benefit plans and the products and services banks provide to these plans, banks also frequently serve as trustees or administrators to employee welfare benefit plans, which are subject to ERISA.

Individuals may establish individual retirement accounts (IRA) to set aside funds for retirement. Banks frequently act as either trustees or custodians to these tax-advantaged accounts authorized under IRC 408.

Retirement plans come in many forms and vary according to the type of benefits provided, the administration of plan assets, income tax treatment, and the method used to determine benefits paid to plan participants and beneficiaries. Refer to appendix A, "Types of Retirement Plans," for more information about the various types of retirement plans.

The OCC, which regulates the federal banking system, has a twofold approach to examining retirement plan products and services. First, the OCC determines whether the bank has identified the material risks associated with the banks' provision of retirement plan products and services. Second, the OCC determines whether the banks' risk management system effectively assesses, measures, monitors, and controls risks associated with providing retirement plan products and services.

Because risk strategies and organizational structures vary, there is no standardized risk management system that works for every bank. Each bank should establish a risk management system suited to its own needs and circumstances.

## Types of Retirement Plan Products and Services

The retirement plan products and services business is complex and competitive. Banks compete with other service providers for the opportunity to provide trustee, investment management, custody, and recordkeeping services to retirement plans. This competition often involves retirement plan consultants or plan sponsors sending out requests for proposals (RFP) to prospective service providers. Service providers then submit proposals to the consultants or plan sponsors. The consultants or plan sponsors choose a service provider based on the information submitted in the RFP.

A bank may provide a full range of retirement plan products and services for employers and individuals and may operate in several capacities when doing so. Examiners and auditors (and others using this booklet) should ascertain in what capacity the bank is acting in regard to a retirement plan and should determine what products or services the bank has agreed to provide the plan. In general, the capacity and a description of the products and services that the bank is providing the plan should be in the service agreement, trust agreement, or other plan documents.

The following capacities represent different levels of fiduciary responsibility:

- A fiduciary with discretionary investment authority, such as investment management.
- A fiduciary with no discretionary investment authority, such as directed trustee.
- A service provider with no discretionary authority, such as recordkeeper.

## Investment Management Services

Banks may provide investment management and advisory services to retirement plans. If a bank exercises any discretionary authority or discretionary control over the management of the plan or over the management or disposition of the plan's assets or renders investment advice on such assets for a fee or other compensation, the bank becomes a fiduciary to the plan. See ERISA 3(21)(A). Compliance with ERISA's fiduciary standards is critical.

For more information related to investment management services, refer to the "Investment Management Services" booklet of the *Comptroller's Handbook*.

## Trustee Services

ERISA requires that all employee benefit plan assets be held in trust and that each plan have at least one named fiduciary. The named fiduciary is generally the plan administrator (which in many cases is also the plan sponsor). The plan's named fiduciary appoints the trustee. Banks may serve as trustees or co-trustees for employee benefit plans. The trustee is a fiduciary with respect to the plan and is responsible for ensuring that the administration of trust assets is proper and complies with plan documents and applicable law. In some cases, one or more persons (employees of the plan sponsor or union members, for example) become the plan's trustee, and a bank may serve in other capacities, such as custodian or agent for the trustees. The plan document and the trust agreement, generally separate documents, establish the various powers, rights, and duties given to the trustee. A trustee may or may not have investment responsibility. Trustees may have different duties or responsibilities for each retirement plan account; trustees' duties and responsibilities are subject to negotiation and established by contract. Plan documents should be carefully examined to determine exactly what the bank's duties and responsibilities are for each retirement plan account.

Retirement plan documents may expressly provide that the trustee is subject to the direction of the named fiduciary, in which case the trustee may be required to take direction from the named fiduciary or a party designated by the named fiduciary, including a third-party investment manager. Trustees become directed trustees in these situations. A directed trustee is required to follow investment directions, if those directions are made in accordance with the terms of the plan and are not contrary to ERISA. Directed trustees must have reasonable processes in place to determine that the directions given, or the actions taken by other fiduciaries, are in accordance with the terms of the plan and are not contrary to ERISA.

# Custody Services

Banks may provide custody services to retirement plans. Typical custody services include settlement, safekeeping, determining the market value of the assets held, and reporting customers' transactions. Under ERISA 3(14)(A), a bank providing custody services is a party in interest with respect to a retirement plan. The bank is not a fiduciary unless the bank as custodian performs a function that is fiduciary in nature. For a discussion of risk management processes regarding custody services, refer to the "Custody Services" booklet of the *Comptroller's Handbook.*

# Participant Recordkeeping Services

Plan sponsors, plan fiduciaries, or named fiduciaries (collectively, plan fiduciaries) generally hire recordkeepers or third-party administrators (TPA) to handle plan administration duties, conduct compliance testing, and maintain participant account information. Recordkeepers and TPAs that act at the direction of the plan fiduciary are typically not fiduciaries to employee benefit plans. Recordkeepers and TPAs generally work closely with the plan trustee to make sure that plan level information reconciles with plan participant level information. The recordkeeper or TPA and the plan fiduciary have a detailed service agreement that specifies the recordkeeper and TPA's duties. Some of the more common processing and advising duties of recordkeepers and TPAs are

- advising the plan fiduciary on regulatory requirements regarding the administration of a plan.
- executing purchases and sales of investment options per participant elections.
- processing participant loan and withdrawal requests.
- processing benefit claims and payment of benefits at the direction of the plan administrator.
- assisting the plan fiduciary with reporting and compliance testing.

Because some plan fiduciaries may not be sufficiently familiar with the rules and regulations governing retirement plans or may not have sufficient resources to handle administration of the plans internally, they hire recordkeepers or TPAs to assist them. Recordkeepers and TPAs help determine who meets the plan's eligibility requirements, the amount of the contributions, and the extent of participants' benefits. Recordkeepers and TPAs may also assist in ensuring that employee benefit plans comply with the numerous laws and regulations governing employee benefit plans.

# Other Products and Services

Examples of other roles a bank might hold in relation to retirement plan products and services include the following:

- Pay benefits to the plan's participants and process withholding tax payments. (See the "Operational Control Processes" section of this booklet for further discussion of benefit payments.)
- Process participant loans from individual account plans that meet ERISA 408(b)(1). (See the "Operational Control Processes" section of this booklet for further discussion of participant loans.)
- Perform compliance testing. Banks may perform testing for compliance with the qualification requirements of the IRC for plans when the bank is also a recordkeeper. Compliance testing may include coverage testing, testing for contribution limits, and "cross-testing" across various age and contribution levels of plan participants to ensure the plans meet participation requirements under part 2 of ERISA and the IRC.
- Provide employee communication material. Banks may provide plan fiduciaries with customized employee communication material that includes education on investments and on the benefits of saving for retirement. Banks may conduct on-site employee meetings.
- Prepare Form 5500.[1] Banks may prepare Form 5500 for a retirement plan. Whether or not they prepare Form 5500, banks as plan service providers generally must provide their direct and indirect compensation to plan fiduciaries in accordance with Schedule C of Form 5500.
- Measure investment performance. Measuring a plan's investment performance involves calculating and reporting the return on the portfolio and various portfolio segments over a specified time. Performance measurement enables the plan fiduciary to compare investment performance with market indices for similar investment styles. For more information on performance measurement, refer to the "Investment Management Services" booklet of the *Comptroller's Handbook*.

# Regulatory Framework

## Internal Revenue Code

Section 401 of the IRC sets strict standards that retirement plans must meet to maintain their qualified status. For example, 401(a)(4) mandates that in order to be a qualified plan, the contributions or benefits provided under the plan must not discriminate in favor of highly compensated individuals. Other requirements under IRC 401 include vesting, distributions, and compensation limits. Plan loans must be made in accordance with IRC 72(p).

---

[1] Form 5500 is the Annual Return/Report of Employee Benefit Plan filed with the DOL to satisfy the plan's annual reporting requirements under title I and title IV of ERISA and the IRC.

# ERISA

ERISA provides rights, protections, safeguards, and guarantees for plan participants and beneficiaries. Numerous amendments have been made to ERISA since its enactment in 1974. This comprehensive federal statute governs the operation and administration of most private sector employee pension and welfare benefit plans. Appendix C contains a summary of the four major sections of ERISA, as well as definitions of commonly used terms. ERISA preempts conflicting state laws that relate to employee benefit plans and effectively establishes a national standard of fiduciary responsibility for persons administering any aspect of a retirement plan. ERISA also contains provisions that authorize the DOL to penalize fiduciaries that breach their fiduciary duties and responsibilities.

ERISA, in accordance with ERISA 4(b), does not apply to governmental plans; church plans; plans maintained solely for the purpose of complying with workmen's compensation laws or unemployment compensation or disability insurance laws; plans maintained outside the United States for the benefit of nonresident aliens; and funded or unfunded excess benefit plans. Governmental plans generally are subject to state laws, which often include fiduciary responsibility provisions similar to ERISA's, or that incorporate ERISA provisions by reference. Refer to appendix C for more information about ERISA and excerpts of its most significant provisions.

## Fiduciary Standards of Care

ERISA imposes a variety of specific duties and responsibilities on institutions and individuals who are fiduciaries, as defined under ERISA 3(21)(A). Having the label of fiduciary does not automatically make an entity or an individual a fiduciary; the actions taken by that entity or individual are the determining factors.

ERISA 404(a) requires fiduciaries to discharge all of their duties with respect to a plan "solely in the interest" of the plan's participants and beneficiaries.

- **Exclusive purpose rule:** 404(a)(1)(A) states that a plan fiduciary must act solely in the interest of the plan's participants and beneficiaries and for the exclusive purpose of providing benefits to participants and their beneficiaries and to defray reasonable expenses of administering the plan.
- **Prudent man rule:** 404(a)(1)(B) states that a fiduciary must act solely in the interest of participants and beneficiaries and "with the care, skill, prudence, and diligence under the circumstances then prevailing that a prudent man acting in a like capacity and familiar with such matters would use in the conduct of an enterprise of like character and with like aim."
- **Diversification:** 404(a)(1)(C) states that a plan fiduciary must act solely in the interest of the plan's participants and beneficiaries by diversifying the investments of the plan so as to minimize the risk of large losses, unless under the circumstances it is clearly prudent not to do so.
- **Compliance with plan documents:** 404(a)(1)(D) states that a plan fiduciary must act solely in the interest of the plan's participants and beneficiaries and in accordance with

- the documents and instruments governing the plan, insofar as they are consistent with ERISA.

Plan fiduciaries that breach any of their fiduciary responsibilities, obligations, or duties imposed by ERISA are personally liable to the plan for any losses the plan suffers because of such breach. The fiduciary must restore to the plan any profits that he or she has made through the use of any plan asset (ERISA 409). Fiduciaries are also subject to other equitable or remedial relief as a court may find appropriate, including removal.

In addition to the previously mentioned broad fiduciary standards of care, ERISA prohibits plan fiduciaries from engaging in very specific transactions referred to as "prohibited transactions." ERISA 406 contains the prohibited transaction rules. Under ERISA 502(i), the DOL may assess a civil penalty against a fiduciary that breaches a fiduciary responsibility, such as engaging in a prohibited transaction. The penalty under 502(i) is equal to 20 percent of the applicable recovery amount paid pursuant to any settlement agreement with the DOL or ordered by a court. The DOL, at its sole discretion, may waive or reduce the penalty (29 CFR 2570.80-88). There is a criminal penalty under ERISA 501 for any person who willfully violates any of the reporting and disclosure provisions under part 1 of ERISA. Upon conviction, the criminal penalty can be a fine of not more than $100,000 or imprisonment for no more than 10 years, or both. If the violation is not by a person, the fine may not exceed $500,000. All cases involving criminal penalties are prosecuted by the U.S. Department of Justice.

Statutory exemptions from the prohibited transaction rules are in ERISA 408. EBSA has the authority to grant individual and class exemptions from the prohibited transaction rules. A number of these exemptions are available for various types of transactions. Unlike individual exemptions, which only offer relief to the specific parties requesting the exemption, class exemptions furnish relief to any parties who engage in transactions of the type covered by the class exemption, if they meet the stated terms and conditions.

IRC 4975 includes virtually identical prohibited transaction rules, except that it uses the term "disqualified person" rather than "party in interest." The penalty provisions under the IRC are more significant from a practical standpoint, as the IRC imposes a two-tiered penalty tax. There is a 15 percent penalty tax on the amount involved in the transaction, and a 100 percent penalty tax on the amount involved if, by a certain date, there is no correction of the prohibited transaction. IRC 4975 applies to IRAs as well as qualified plans.

For more information, refer to appendix D, "Prohibited Transactions."

# Risks Associated With Retirement Plan Products and Services

From a supervisory perspective, risk is the potential that events, expected or unexpected, will have an adverse effect on a bank's earnings, capital, or franchise or enterprise value. The OCC has defined eight categories of risk for bank supervision purposes: credit, interest rate, liquidity, price, operational, compliance, strategic, and reputation. These categories are not mutually exclusive. Any product or service may expose a bank to multiple risks. Risks also may be interdependent and may be positively or negatively correlated. Examiners should be aware of this interdependence and assess the effect in a consistent and inclusive manner. Refer to the "Bank Supervision Process" booklet of the *Comptroller's Handbook* for an expanded discussion of banking risks and their definitions.

Banks that provide retirement plan products and services are subject to many types of risks. The following sections address these risks from the perspective of the OCC's risk assessment system. Generally, compliance, operational, strategic, and reputation risks are associated with retirement plan products and services.

## Compliance Risk

Compliance risk is a substantial factor in the overall risk framework for retirement plan products and services. Compliance risk encompasses not only compliance with applicable laws and regulations but also adherence to sound fiduciary principles, prudent ethical standards, specifications in client documents, and internal policies and procedures. A bank that does not comply with the prohibited transaction rules must correct the transactions and may be required to pay a civil penalty. Even if the amount involved in a prohibited transaction is relatively small, civil penalties can amount to substantial sums. If the administration of a retirement plan or IRA does not conform to IRS and DOL requirements, the plan is at risk of losing its tax-exempt status and the plan's assets become taxable income to the participant or IRA owner. Income taxes and penalties may apply. Corrective action may also be required. If the bank's actions, or its failure to act, contribute to such results, the liability to the bank could be substantial. A bank that does not comply with applicable law can also be subject to litigation, regulatory action, and damage to its reputation. While the financial impact for any specific compliance failure is often difficult to estimate, it can be significant in relation to the bank's earnings and capital.

Banks should pay particular attention to compliance with the statutory exceptions from the definition of "broker" in section 3(a)(4) of the Securities Exchange Act of 1934 that was established in title II of the Gramm–Leach–Bliley Act (GLBA). Title II of the GLBA repealed the blanket exemption from broker registration that previously applied to banks' securities activities and established several specific exceptions for certain securities activities that banks may engage in without being considered a broker. For other securities activities, unless the bank registers with the U.S. Securities and Exchange Commission (SEC) as a broker, the bank must "push out" the activities to a registered affiliate or third-party brokerage firm subject to SEC regulation. The implementing regulations that define the extent to which securities brokerage activities of banks are subject to SEC regulation are the Federal Reserve Board regulations at 12 CFR 218 (Regulation R) and the SEC regulations at 17 CFR 247 (Regulation R). Banks that are trustee to employee benefit plans should pay particular attention to the trust activities statutory exception as well as the regulations relating to the chiefly compensated test at 12 CFR 218.721-723 and 17 CFR 247.721-723. Banks that are acting as a custodian to employee benefit plans should pay particular attention to the safekeeping and custody statutory exception as well as 12 CFR 218.760 and 17 CFR 247.760.

The "Asset Management" booklet of the *Comptroller's Handbook* discusses the statutory exceptions to the definition of "broker" for banks that transact securities for the accounts of others as well as the exemptions in Regulation R.

Banks should also pay particular attention to their Bank Secrecy Act/Anti-Money Laundering (BSA/AML) compliance programs as they relate to the banks' provisions of employee benefit products and services. The bank's account acceptance process for employee benefit plans should include an effective customer identification program. The bank's employee benefit plan accounts should be included in the bank's BSA/AML monitoring program. Finally, distributions from employee benefit plans and IRA accounts should comply with Office of Foreign Assets Control (OFAC) regulations and be included in the bank's OFAC compliance program.

For more information on BSA/AML and OFAC compliance programs, refer to the Federal Financial Institutions Examination Council's (FFIEC) *Bank Secrecy Act/Anti-Money Laundering Examination Manual.*

Managing compliance risk associated with retirement plan products and services requires specialized expertise in a challenging and ever-changing regulatory environment. ERISA and the IRC are complex statutes and subject to frequent revision and interpretation in the form of legislation, regulation, and DOL and IRS issuances. Some factors that could raise the bank's level of compliance risk include the following:

- Deficient account acceptance processes.
- Deficient investment and administrative review processes.
- Lack of effective procedures for administration of complex assets (such as derivatives) or higher risk assets (such as employer stock).
- Lack of knowledge and weaknesses in training programs.
- Weak internal audit and compliance management functions.
- Failure to consult legal counsel when appropriate.

# Operational Risk

Operational risk is inherent in the delivery of products and services to retirement plans. A bank may process large volumes of many types of transactions that require a high degree of accuracy. Sound internal control processes are required. Operational risk increases when a bank offers participant recordkeeping services. The volume of transactions at a participant level is exponentially higher than at the plan level. A bank must have the appropriate tools to reconcile participant level transactions, such as mutual fund purchases and sales, with plan level transactions. Also critical is the timely allocation of receipts, such as contributions and income on investments, to participant accounts. Plan level totals must be reconciled with the individual participant accounts. Allocation errors at any level can be difficult and time consuming to correct.

The information systems necessary to properly provide products and services to retirement plans are costly to acquire. Updates to the information systems must occur in response to regulatory changes. Participant recordkeeping requires a complex system that is typically distinct from the core trust accounting system. Benefit payment systems and certified reporting packages are examples of other systems the bank may use to support retirement plan products and services, regardless of whether it offers recordkeeping services. Some factors that could raise the bank's level of operational risk include the following:

- Use of manual (rather than automated) information systems.
- Inadequate information systems.
- Deficient processes and controls within the information system related to
    - plan contributions.
    - participant distributions.
    - payment of plan expenses.
    - securities related transactions.
    - tax withholding and reporting.
    - valuation of retirement plan assets.
    - failure to timely provide plan fiduciaries with required service provider fee disclosures.
- Inadequate disaster recovery planning.
- Fraud or defalcations.
- Failure to effectively manage third-party vendor relationships.

## Strategic Risk

The provision of retirement plan products and services can be an important component of bank profitability and shareholder value. Financial success requires a sound strategic planning process embraced by the board of directors and senior management. Because the regulatory environment is complex and dedicated processing systems are costly, providing retirement plan products and services requires a substantial and long-term commitment. Some examples of factors that could raise a bank's level of strategic risk include the following:

- Failure to provide adequate resources to the retirement plan products and services line of business and related control functions.
- Lack of sufficient scale to operate at a profitable level.
- Weaknesses in the administration of acquisitions, mergers, and alliances.

## Reputation Risk

A good reputation is essential to success in the retirement plan products and services marketplace. Competition for retirement plan customers is intense. Negative publicity, deserved or not, can damage a bank's ability to compete. A strong reputation is essential to attract and retain business. A bank's reputation may be enhanced by having state-of-the-art products and services, competitive investment performance, high-quality customer service, and compliance with applicable law. Some factors that could raise an institution's level of reputation risk include the following:

- Errors in processing and poor customer service.
- Poor investment performance or lack of a clear and consistently applied investment management philosophy.
- Violations of applicable law or regulation, regulatory enforcement action, litigation, or other negative publicity.
- Lack of a strong ethical culture and internal control environment.
- Sales practices that are incompatible with fiduciary responsibilities.
- The bank's ability to provide the agreed-upon services.

# Assessment of Risk Management

The OCC expects each bank to identify, measure, monitor, and control risk by implementing an effective risk management system appropriate for its size and the complexity of its operations. When examiners assess the effectiveness of a bank's risk management system, they consider the bank's policies, processes, personnel, and control systems. Refer to the "Bank Supervision Process" booklet of the *Comptroller's Handbook* for an expanded discussion of risk management.

# Board and Management Supervision

A bank's board is ultimately responsible for the bank's provision of retirement plan products and services (for national banks 12 CFR 9.4, for federal savings associations 12 CFR 150.150). The board may assign authority for the management of retirement plan products and services to bank officers, specific directors, employees, or committees. Whoever has the board's authority must keep the board adequately informed about risk identification and risk management in the bank retirement plan products and services line of business and be responsible for the implementation, integrity, and maintenance of the risk management system. Other responsibilities include the following:

- Ensuring implementation of the bank's strategy.
- Developing policies that define the bank's risk appetite and ensuring those risks are compatible with strategic goals.
- Ensuring that strategic direction and risk appetite are effectively communicated and adhered to throughout the organization.
- Overseeing the development and maintenance of a management information system to ensure that information is timely, accurate, and complete.

## Strategic Planning

Increasing competition and the dynamic nature of the financial services industry demands strategic planning and monitoring. The board is responsible for approving the bank's strategic asset management goals and objectives and for providing the necessary managerial, financial, technological, and organizational resources to achieve those goals and objectives. The board and management must understand that offering certain retirement plan products and services, such as participant recordkeeping, require a significant and ongoing investment in technology.

## Management

The board is responsible for the selection of an experienced and competent employee benefits management team. Management succession planning and ongoing educational programs are essential given the industry's competitive nature, employee mobility, and frequency of changes in statutory and regulatory requirements.

## Policies

The board, or its designated committee(s), must adopt policies that promote sound risk management processes. Policies should promote ethical practices and avoidance of prohibited transactions. Strong internal controls, a sound audit coverage, and an appropriate management information system complement policies. The board or its designated committee(s) should review policies annually and revise them when appropriate.

Policies should provide management with guidance concerning the types of retirement plan products and services and level of risk acceptable to management. At a minimum, this guidance should define and describe

- types of retirement plans the bank generally accepts (e.g., defined benefit plans, defined contribution plans, employee stock ownership plans (ESOP), 401(k) plans).
- services the bank offers (e.g., trustee, investment manager, custodian, or recordkeeping).
- target size of retirement plans the bank accepts.
- types of assets the bank accepts as plan investments (e.g., readily marketable securities, employer securities, real estate, closely held securities, and hard-to-value assets).

Management must also ensure that the bank is positioned to collect fees that are commensurate with the costs and risks associated with its retirement plan products and services. The bank must take into account ERISA and the IRC in determining how to receive its fees.

## Product and Service Development

In developing and implementing strategies for retirement plan products and services, management must establish a uniform process for assessing the risk of new retirement plan products and services. See OCC Bulletin 2004-20, "Risk Management of New, Expanded, or Modified Bank Products and Services: Risk Management Process." The approval process for new products or services should include reviews by risk management, operations, accounting, legal, audit, and business-line management, as applicable. The evaluation and testing of new products, services, and distribution channels before full implementation is critical. Depending on the significance of the new product or service and its impact on the bank's risk profile, senior management, and in some cases the board, should provide the final approval.

## Third-Party Service Providers

To deliver retirement plan products and services, banks increasingly need third-party relationships to provide technology, administrative, and operational services. A bank's use of third parties does not diminish the responsibility of its board and senior management to ensure that the activity is performed in a safe and sound manner and in compliance with applicable law.[2]

A bank should adopt risk management processes commensurate with the level of risk and complexity of its third-party relationships and the bank's organizational structure. Therefore, the OCC expects more comprehensive and rigorous oversight and management of third-party relationships that involve critical activities. Critical activities are those that involve significant bank functions (e.g., payments, clearing, settlements, and custody) or significant shared services (e.g., information technology), or other activities that

- could cause a bank to face significant risk if the third party fails to meet expectations.
- could have significant customer impacts.
- require significant investment in resources to implement the third-party relationship and manage the risk.
- could have a major impact on bank operations if the bank has to find an alternative third party or if the outsourced activity has to be brought in-house.

An effective third-party risk management process follows a continuous life cycle for all relationships and incorporates the following phases:

- **Planning:** Developing a plan to manage the relationship is often the first step in the third-party risk management process. This step is helpful in many situations but is necessary when a bank is considering contracts with third parties that involve critical activities.
- **Due diligence and third-party selection:** Conducting a review of a potential third party before signing a contract helps ensure that the bank selects an appropriate third party and understands and controls the risks posed by the relationship, consistent with the bank's risk appetite.
- **Contract negotiation:** Developing a contract that clearly defines expectations and responsibilities of the third party helps to ensure the contract's enforceability, limit the bank's liability, and mitigate disputes about performance.
- **Ongoing monitoring:** Performing ongoing monitoring of the third-party relationship once the contract is in place is essential to the bank's ability to manage risk of the third-party relationship.
- **Termination:** Developing a contingency plan to ensure that the bank can transition the activities to another third party, bring the activities in-house, or discontinue the activities

---

[2] OCC Bulletin 2013-29, "Third-Party Relationships: Risk Management Guidance."

when a contract expires, the terms of the contract have been satisfied, in response to contract default, or in response to changes to the bank's or third party's business strategy.

In addition, banks should perform the following throughout the life cycle of the relationship as part of its risk management process:

- **Oversight and accountability:** Assigning clear roles and responsibilities for managing third-party relationships and integrating the bank's third-party risk management process with its enterprise risk management framework enables continuous oversight and accountability.
- **Documentation and reporting:** Proper documentation and reporting facilitates oversight, accountability, monitoring, and risk management associated with third-party relationships.
- **Independent reviews:** Conducting periodic independent reviews of the risk management process enables management to assess whether the process aligns with the bank's strategy and effectively manages risk posed by third-party relationships. The bank's internal auditor or an independent third party may perform the reviews, and senior management should ensure that the results are reported to the board.

## Indemnification and Liability Insurance

ERISA 410(a) provides that any provision in a plan document or agreement that "purports to relieve a fiduciary from responsibility or liability for any responsibility, obligation, or duty … shall be void as against public policy." An indemnification agreement that leaves a fiduciary fully responsible and liable, but which permits another party to satisfy any liability incurred by the fiduciary in the same manner as insurance, however, is not void under 29 CFR 2509.75-4, Interpretive Bulletin (IB) 75-4.

The DOL interprets ERISA 410(a) as rendering void any arrangement for indemnification of a fiduciary of an employee benefit plan by the plan. Such an arrangement would have the same result as an exculpatory clause, in that it would, in effect, relieve the fiduciary of responsibility and liability to the plan by abrogating the plan's right to recovery from the fiduciary for breaches of fiduciary obligations. A provision in an agreement is void, therefore, if the agreement provides indemnification of a plan fiduciary by the plan following a breach of duties. The DOL's Advisory Opinion (AO) 2002-08A, August 20, 2002, addresses whether the inclusion of limitation of liability and indemnification provisions in a service provider contract would violate ERISA's fiduciary provisions. The DOL concludes that provisions that purport to apply to fraud or willful misconduct by the service provider are void as against public policy but other limitations of liability and indemnification provisions, applying to negligence and unintentional malpractice, may be consistent with ERISA when considered in connection with the reasonableness of the arrangement as a whole and the potential risks to participants and beneficiaries.

ERISA 410(b) permits (but does not require) fiduciaries to be covered by fiduciary liability insurance.

# Account Acceptance and Reviews

## Pre-Acceptance Reviews

Banks are required to review a prospective fiduciary account before accepting the account (for national banks 12 CFR 9.6(a), for federal savings associations 12 CFR 150.200). As part of the pre-acceptance review process, the bank should determine whether it has the expertise and systems to properly manage the account and whether the account meets the bank's risk and profitability standards. The pre-acceptance review should consider the type of account, governing documents, required products or services, and the assets held in the account. Appropriately documented records of accounts accepted or declined should be in the bank's records. The bank's counsel (internal or external) should review any nonproprietary or customized plan documents for an account before acceptance.

The pre-acceptance review process continues after the bank submits a bid in response to an RFP. Before the bank accepts the retirement account, the bank has the opportunity to assess the risk associated with each requested service, review the prospective account for compliance with internal policy, and determine whether the fee the bank receives is commensurate with the services the bank intends to provide.

## Establishment of Accounts

Account administrators often use checklists to ensure they obtain all the information needed to establish an account. These checklists usually itemize all the documents required to open an account (governing document, asset schedules, fee schedules, etc.). It is common to prepare synoptic records during account setup. These records summarize the documents that state the bank's capacity and responsibilities and summarize the account's investment policy statement. The bank's trust accounting system typically contains this type of information. If synoptic records are utilized, then the bank should establish a periodic process to ensure that the synoptic records are accurate (e.g., during annual administrative reviews). Other banks may choose not to utilize synoptic records and instead work from the original documents.

Retirement plan assets are deposited into an account once the account is formally established. The operations department is responsible for establishing controls to ensure the receipt of the plan's assets is properly reflected on the account inventory and appropriate accounting entries are made. If the bank provides participant recordkeeping services, the bank must have a process for converting and balancing records at the participant level as well as at the account or retirement plan level.

## Account Reviews

After acceptance of a retirement plan for which the bank has investment discretion, such as a defined benefit plan, the bank must, in accordance with 12 CFR 9.6(b) for national banks and 12 CFR 150.210 for federal savings associations, promptly review all the plan assets to evaluate whether the assets are appropriate for the account. The appropriateness of each asset depends on the investment objective of the account. An investment policy statement contains the account's investment objectives and strategies. Refer to the "Investment Management Services" booklet of the *Comptroller's Handbook* for more information on investment policy statements.

Under 12 CFR 9.6(c) for national banks and 12 CFR 150.220 for federal savings associations, the bank must review, at least once during each calendar year, all assets in each fiduciary account for which it has investment discretion. Account reviews of retirement plans for which the bank has investment discretion must determine whether assets are appropriate, individually and collectively, for the account. During the review, the bank should analyze investment performance and should require the plan fiduciary to confirm or update the account's investment policy statement, including asset allocation guidelines. For more information, see OCC Bulletin 2008-10, "Fiduciary Activities of National Banks: Annual Reviews of Fiduciary Accounts Pursuant to 12 CFR 9.6(c)."

Completing periodic administrative account reviews is a sound risk management practice. An administrative account review helps to determine whether coding and other account information is accurate. Such reviews also help determine whether account administration is in accordance with governing instruments and the bank's policies and procedures. Administrative reviews are good opportunities to evaluate service quality and consider whether to expand the retirement plan products and services line of business. In some banks, administrative officers complete these reviews and submit the findings to an appropriate fiduciary committee. Other banks may have a different administrative review process. The structure of the administrative review process should fit the organization's risk and compliance management process, as well as the bank's products and services.

# ERISA Compliance Issues

### Fiduciary Responsibilities of Directed Trustees

A trustee, under ERISA 402(c)(3), has the exclusive authority and discretion to manage plan assets, unless the plan expressly provides that the trustee is subject to the direction of a named fiduciary who is not a trustee. In these situations, the trustee is a directed trustee and should make sure that the directions it receives are in accordance with the terms of the plan and are not contrary to ERISA.

Under ERISA, even though directed trustees are fiduciaries to retirement plans, their responsibilities are narrower than that of trustees with investment discretion (Field Assistance Bulletin (FAB) 2004-03, "Fiduciary Responsibilities of Directed Trustees"). Under ERISA 403(a)(1), a directed trustee is subject to the proper directions of a named fiduciary. A direction is proper only if the direction is

- made in accordance with the terms of the plan **and**
- not contrary to ERISA.

Under FAB 2004-03, when a directed trustee knows or should know that a direction from a named fiduciary is not made in accordance with the terms of the plan, or is contrary to

ERISA, the directed trustee may not, consistent with its fiduciary responsibilities, follow the direction.

To determine whether directions received from a plan fiduciary are in accordance with the terms of the plan, a directed trustee has a duty to request and review all the documents and instruments governing the plan that are relevant to the directed trustee's duties. If a directed trustee either fails to request the plan documents or fails to review the documents and, as a result of such failure, follows a direction contrary to the terms of the plan, the directed trustee may be liable for following such direction. A directed trustee has a duty to request and review pertinent plan documents and, therefore, should know that the direction was not in accordance with the terms of the plan. If a directed trustee follows an improper direction, as would be the case when the purchase of a particular stock at the direction of the plan's named fiduciary is contrary to the plan's investment policy, the directed trustee may be liable for a breach of its fiduciary duty to follow only proper directions.

FAB 2004-03 states that it is the DOL's view that a direction is consistent with the terms of a plan if the documents pursuant to which the plan is established and operated do not prohibit the direction. If, in the course of reviewing the propriety of a particular direction, a directed trustee determines that the terms of the relevant documents are ambiguous with respect to the permissibility of the direction, the directed trustee should obtain a clarification of the plan terms from the fiduciary responsible for interpreting such terms to ensure that the direction is proper.

Even when a direction is consistent with the terms of the plan, the direction may nonetheless fail to be a proper direction because it is contrary to ERISA. Under ERISA 403(a)(1), a directed trustee may not follow a direction that the trustee knows or should know is contrary to ERISA. For example, the directed trustee may not follow a direction that would require the trustee to engage in a prohibited transaction or would violate the prudence requirement of section 404(a)(1). A bank as a directed trustee must follow policies and procedures that are designed to avoid prohibited transactions. A directed trustee could satisfy this obligation by obtaining appropriate written representations from the directing fiduciary that the plan maintains and follows procedures for identifying prohibited transactions and, if prohibited, identifying the individual or class exemption applicable to the transaction. The bank, as directed trustee, may rely on the representations of the directing fiduciary unless the directed trustee knows that the representations are false.

Under FAB 2004-03, a directed trustee does not have an independent obligation to determine the prudence of every transaction. The directed trustee also does not have an obligation to duplicate or second-guess the work of the plan fiduciaries that have discretionary authority over the management of plan assets.

The directed trustee's obligation to question market transactions involving publicly traded stock on prudence grounds is quite limited. The primary circumstance in which a directed trustee may have such an obligation is when the directed trustee possesses material, nonpublic information regarding a security. If a directed trustee has material nonpublic information that is necessary for a prudent decision, the directed trustee, before following a direction that would be affected by such information, has a duty to inquire about the named fiduciary's knowledge and consideration of the information with respect to the direction. For example, if a directed trustee has nonpublic information indicating that a company's public financial statements contain material misrepresentations that significantly inflate the company's earnings, the trustee could not simply follow a direction to purchase the company's stock at an artificially inflated price. Generally, the possession of nonpublic information by one part of the bank is not imputed to the entire bank if the bank maintains a Chinese Wall or similar procedures designed to restrict the flow of information between the various parts of the bank under banking and securities laws.

Under FAB 2004-03, absent material, nonpublic information, a directed trustee rarely has an obligation under ERISA to question the prudence of a direction to purchase publicly traded securities at the market price solely on the basis of publicly available information. In limited, extraordinary circumstances, where there are clear and compelling public indicators—as evidenced by an 8-K filing with the SEC, a bankruptcy filing, or similar public indicator— that call into serious question a company's viability as a going concern, the directed trustee may have a duty not to follow the named fiduciary's instruction without further inquiry. If, however, an independent fiduciary were appointed to manage the plan's investment in company stock, a directed trustee could follow the proper directions of the independent fiduciary without having to conduct its own independent assessment of the transaction.

## Co-Fiduciary Liability

Under certain circumstances, banks as plan fiduciaries may be liable for a breach of fiduciary duty even if the bank plays no direct role in the activity causing the breach. Banks whose services make them fiduciaries must be aware of the activities of co-fiduciaries and have adequate processes in place to manage the risks associated with the services that co-fiduciaries provide. Banks should have policies in place that require consultation with ERISA counsel in co-fiduciary situations to assess the potential for liability.

Under ERISA 405(a), a bank may be held liable for a co-fiduciary's breach in the following situations.

- **Knowing participation:** A bank knowingly participates in, or knowingly undertakes to conceal, an act or omission of the other fiduciary, knowing the act or omission to be a breach of fiduciary responsibility.
- **Enabling a breach:** By failure to comply with its fiduciary duties, the bank has enabled the other fiduciary to commit a breach of fiduciary responsibility.
- **Duty to remedy a breach:** Having knowledge of a breach by the other fiduciary, the bank makes no reasonable efforts under the circumstances to remedy the breach of fiduciary responsibility.

In accordance with FAB 2004-03, and under ERISA 405(a)(1), a bank would be liable for the breach of fiduciary responsibility of a co-fiduciary if the bank "participates knowingly" in the breach of the co-fiduciary. Accordingly, if a bank as directed trustee has knowledge of a breach of fiduciary responsibility, the bank may be liable unless the bank takes reasonable steps to remedy the breach. A bank trustee should not follow directions from the named fiduciary if it knows that the named fiduciary is failing to discharge its obligations in accordance with ERISA's requirements. Efforts to remedy a breach (or to prevent an imminent breach) may include reporting the breach to other fiduciaries of the plan or to the DOL.

Under ERISA 405(d)(1), directed trustees are generally relieved of co-fiduciary liability for following investment directions from a properly appointed investment manager that meets the qualification requirements set forth in ERISA 3(38). Under ERISA 3(38), an investment manager must be a registered investment adviser, a bank, or an insurance company **and** must have acknowledged in writing that it is a fiduciary with respect to the plan.

## Managing Prohibited Transactions

All qualified plans are subject to the prohibited transaction rules found in ERISA. IRAs are subject to the prohibited transaction rules found in the IRC that are similar, but not identical, to ERISA's prohibited transaction rules. ERISA's rules affect parties in interest and the IRC's rules affect disqualified persons. The two terms are substantially the same in most respects, but ERISA's definition of parties in interest is slightly broader than the definition of disqualified persons. The pertinent rules are in ERISA 406 and IRC 4975.

Banks should develop policies and procedures that prevent the bank from entering into prohibited transactions. The policies and procedures should also provide guidance on transactions or situations that are subject to a statutory prohibited transaction exemption, an individual prohibited transaction exemption, or a prohibited transaction class exemption (PTE) to make sure that all terms and conditions of the exemption are met. Unlike individual exemptions, which only offer relief to the specific parties requesting the exemptions, class exemptions furnish relief to any parties who engage in transactions of the type covered by the class exemption, if they meet the stated terms and conditions.

Appendix D contains details on the statutory exemptions and PTEs most often used by banks.

Because the prohibited transaction rules and the various exemptions are complex, bank employees must receive initial training and continuing education. The execution of policies and procedures in this area should be monitored and included in an audit review.

## Section 404(c) Plans

ERISA 404(c) relieves plan fiduciaries (including trustees) from losses that result from a participant's investment elections, if certain conditions are met. If an individual account plan (typically a 401(k) plan) permits participants to choose, among the available plan investments, how to invest the assets in his or her account, then the plan fiduciary (including the trustee) shall not be liable for losses, which result from the participant or beneficiary's investment choices. All the conditions stated in ERISA 404(c) must be met to make this relief available. Fiduciaries are not, however, relieved from liability for matters that are not a result of the participant's investment choices.

ERISA does not require that plans comply with the requirements of ERISA 404(c). Noncompliance only means that plan fiduciaries remain liable for losses resulting from participants' investment choices. Guidance on how a plan can meet each of the three main components of ERISA 404(c) is at 29 CFR 2550.404c-1.

## Automatic Enrollment

Plan fiduciaries may ask banks to help them set up an automatic enrollment employee benefit plan under ERISA 404(c)(5) (and the implementing regulations at 29 CFR 2550.404c-5) or to provide services to these plans. There are some differences among the various types of automatic enrollment plans. Banks should thoroughly understand the default investment options that, if used, can limit some of the liability of plan fiduciaries.

The DOL and the IRS have jointly published a booklet titled "Automatic Enrollment 401(k) Plans for Small Businesses." The booklet is very helpful and is available on the EBSA Web site at www.dol.gov/ebsa. These plans are growing in popularity among businesses of all sizes.

- **A basic automatic enrollment 401(k) plan** automatically enrolls employees unless they elect otherwise. The plan specifies the percentage of automatic deduction from each employee's paycheck for contribution to the plan. The plan document must also explain that employees have the right to decline having salary deferrals withheld or to elect a different withholding percentage.
- **An eligible automatic contribution arrangement** (EACA) is similar to the basic automatic enrollment plan but has specific notice requirements. An EACA can allow automatically enrolled participants to withdraw their contributions within 30 to 90 days of the first contribution.
- **A qualified automatic contribution arrangement** (QACA) is a type of automatic enrollment 401(k) plan that passes annual discrimination testing. The plan must include certain features, such as a fixed schedule of automatic employee contributions, employer contributions, a special vesting schedule, and specific notice requirements.

There are regulations at 29 CFR 2550.404c-5 that provide detailed conditions that, if met, allow plan fiduciaries to limit their liability for any loss that is the direct and necessary result of investing all or part of a participant's or beneficiary's account in any qualified default investment alternatives. The conditions to obtain this relief from liability include the following:

- Plan fiduciaries place the participants' contributions in qualified default investment alternatives (QDIA) described in 29 CFR 2550.404c-5(e) and discussed in more detail in the next paragraph.
- Before the deposit of a participant's first contribution, the participant receives a notice describing the automatic enrollment process and the QDIA. Participants are sent a similar notice annually thereafter. The notice must meet certain requirements described in 29 CFR 2550.404c-5(d).
- The participant has the opportunity to provide investment direction but does not.

- The plan passes along to the participant or beneficiary material related to the investment, such as a prospectus.
- The participant has a periodic opportunity to direct his or her investments from the default investment to a broad range of other options.

**Qualified Default Investment Alternatives**

Plan fiduciaries are relieved from liability under automatic enrollment plans if the default investments meet certain criteria. Plan fiduciaries can choose from four types of qualified default investment alternatives for employees' automatic contributions. Three alternatives minimize the risk of large losses and provide long-term growth through diversification. All four types, briefly summarized, are as follows.

1. An investment fund product or an investment portfolio with an investment mix that changes asset allocation and risk, based on the employee's age, projected retirement date, or life expectancy (for example, a life cycle or target date fund).
2. An investment fund product or model portfolio with an investment mix designed to provide long-term appreciation and capital preservation through a mix of equity and fixed-income exposures, consistent with a target level of risk appropriate for plan participants as a whole (for example, a balanced fund).
3. An investment management service that spreads contributions among plan options to provide an asset mix that takes into account the individual's age, projected retirement date, or life expectancy (for example, a professionally managed account).
4. Solely, for amounts invested for the first 120 days of a participant's contributions, a product or fund designed to preserve principal and provide a reasonable rate of return, whether or not the return is guaranteed, consistent with liquidity. The fund should seek to maintain, over the term of the investment, the dollar value that is equal to the amount invested. A state or federally regulated financial institution must offer the fund.

These alternatives can include products offered through variable annuity contracts and other pooled investment funds, such as bank collective investment funds. Default investments cannot include employer securities unless the employer securities are in a mutual fund or a bank collective investment fund under certain conditions.

## Investment Advice and Investment Education

The growth of participant-directed retirement plans has led to increasing demand for assistance to participants as they invest their account balances. Concerns that such assistance may be viewed as providing investment advice, however, have caused plan fiduciaries to resist providing assistance to participants in participant-directed plans.

Many plan fiduciaries have, however, chosen to provide plan participants and beneficiaries with investment educational materials. EBSA clarified the difference between investment education and investment advice in IB 96-1, which can be found at 29 CFR 2509.96-1.

Under IB 96-1, furnishing the following categories of information and materials to a participant or beneficiary in a participant-directed individual account plan does not constitute the rendering of investment advice irrespective of who provides the information, the frequency with which the information is shared, the form in which the information and materials are provided, or whether the information from one category is furnished with information from another category. The categories are the following:

- Plan information
- General financial and investment information
- Asset allocation models
- Interactive investment materials

EBSA has issued regulations at 29 CFR 2550.408g-1, which provide more guidance on the statutory exemptions from prohibited transaction violations at ERISA 408(b)(14) and 408(g) regarding the provision of investment advice to participants and beneficiaries in individual account plans, such as 401(k) plans and IRAs.

The regulation provides relief from the prohibitions of ERISA 406 and IRC 4975 for certain transactions in connection with the provision of investment advice to participants and beneficiaries if the bank uses an "eligible investment advice arrangement." An eligible investment advice arrangement

- uses fee leveling as described in 29 CFR 2550.408g-1(b)(3).
- uses computer models as described in 29 CFR 2550.408g-1(b)(4).
- meets the conditions in the regulation pertinent to both methods.

The regulation allows banks that provide investment advice to use computer models developed by the banks, under certain conditions, rather than models developed by independent parties.

Most importantly, the regulation retains as effective all previously issued regulations, exemptions, interpretive bulletins, and advisory letters that relate to the provision of investment advice. Some of the previously issued guidance include the following.

- **FAB 2007-01.** The FAB affirmed that the enactment of the new statutory exemption (408(g)) did not invalidate or otherwise affect prior guidance relating to investment advice. The FAB also reiterated that a plan sponsor may use plan assets to pay for a contract with an independent investment adviser (that is not affiliated with a fiduciary) to offer investment advice to plan participants and beneficiaries. An example would be the hire of "Financial Engines." This company is independent of any bank, broker-dealer, or registered investment adviser.
- **AO 2001-09A.** Under the Sun America AO, individual investment decisions or recommendations provided or implemented under a model asset allocation computer program that applies a methodology developed, maintained, and overseen by a financial expert independent of the investment adviser are not prohibited transactions.

- **AOs 97-15A and 2005-10A.** If a bank is a fiduciary by virtue of being a directed trustee, the bank's affiliate (most likely a registered investment adviser) may provide investment advice to the plan participants without engaging in a prohibited transaction if the fees of the fiduciary investment adviser do not vary or are offset against those received by the bank for the provision of investment advice.
- **IB 96-1:** This IB identifies categories of investment-related information and materials that do not constitute investment advice.

## Fee Disclosures

### Service Provider Fee Disclosure Regulation

ERISA requires plan fiduciaries, when selecting and monitoring service providers (such as banks), to act prudently and solely in the interest of the plan's participants and beneficiaries. Plan fiduciaries also must ensure that arrangements with banks and other service providers are "reasonable" and that service providers receive only reasonable compensation. Fundamental to the ability of plan fiduciaries to discharge these obligations is to obtain sufficient information to enable them to make informed decisions regarding service providers, such as the costs and extent of the provided services as well as how much compensation service providers receive.

In recent years, compensation arrangements for service providers (e.g., through revenue-sharing and other arrangements) have become increasingly complex. Many of these changes have improved efficiency and reduced the costs of administrative services and benefits for plans and their participants. The complexity has made it difficult, however, for plan fiduciaries to understand how much compensation service providers are receiving and how they are receiving it. To combat this problem, EBSA issued the 408(b)(2) regulation (29 CFR 2550.408b-2). This regulation establishes specific disclosure obligations for banks and other service providers.

The regulation applies to ERISA-covered, defined benefit, and defined contribution pension plans. The regulation does not apply to simplified employee pension plans (SEP), savings incentive match plan for employees (SIMPLE) retirement accounts, IRAs, certain annuity contracts and custodial accounts described in IRC 403(b), or employee welfare benefit plans.

In accordance with the 408(b)(2) regulation, banks and other service providers who expect to receive at least $1,000 in compensation, referred to as covered service providers (CSP), are required to provide plan fiduciaries, in writing, certain information.

The following summarizes the 408(b)(2) requirements. See 408(b)(2) for complete details. CSPs are to provide plan fiduciaries with the following:

- **Services:** A description of the services to be provided to the plan pursuant to the contract or arrangement.
- **Status:** A statement as to whether the CSP is a fiduciary.

- **Compensation:** A description of all direct and indirect compensation received by the CSP and its affiliates or subcontractors. Compensation consists of the following categories:
    1. **Direct compensation**: Compensation received directly from the plan.
    2. **Indirect compensation:** Compensation received from any source other than the plan, plan sponsor, CSP, or an affiliate. Compensation received from a subcontractor is indirect compensation, unless it is received in connection with services performed under the subcontractor's contract or arrangement. CSPs must also provide an identification of the services for which the indirect compensation will be received, identification of the payer of the indirect compensation, and a description of the arrangement between the payer and the CSP, an affiliate, or a subcontractor pursuant to which indirect compensation is paid.
    3. **Compensation paid among related parties:** Compensation that will be paid among the CSP, an affiliate, or a subcontractor in connection with the services provided if it is set on a transaction basis (e.g., commissions, soft dollars, finder's fees or other similar incentive compensation based on business placed or retained) or is charged directly against the plan's investment and reflected in the net value of the investment (e.g., Rule 12b-1 fees); including identification of the services for which such compensation will be paid and identification of the payers and recipients of such compensation (including the status of a payer or recipient as an affiliate or a subcontractor).
    4. **Compensation for termination of contract or arrangement:** Compensation that the CSP, an affiliate, or a subcontractor reasonably expects to receive in connection with termination of the contract or arrangement, and how any prepaid amounts will be calculated and refunded upon such termination.
- **Recordkeeping services:** A description of all direct and indirect compensation that the CSP, an affiliate, or a subcontractor reasonably expects to receive in connection with the recordkeeping services. If the CSP reasonably expects recordkeeping services to be provided, in whole or in part, without explicit compensation for these services or when compensation for recordkeeping services is offset or rebated based on other compensation received by the CSP, an affiliate, or a subcontractor, a reasonable and good faith estimate of the cost to the CSP of the recordkeeping services must be disclosed. The disclosure should include an explanation of the methodology and assumptions used to prepare the estimate and a detailed explanation of the recordkeeping services that will be provided. The estimate should take into account the rates that the CSP, an affiliate, or a subcontractor would charge to, or be paid by, third parties, or the prevailing market rates charged, for similar recordkeeping services for a similar plan with a similar number of participants and beneficiaries.
- **Investment disclosure—fiduciary services:** The CSP must disclose, with respect to each investment contract, product, or entity that holds plan assets and in which the plan has a direct equity investment, and for which fiduciary services will be provided, the following:
    1. A description of any compensation that will be charged directly against an investment, such as commissions, sales loads, sales charges, deferred sales charges, redemption fees, surrender charges, exchange fees, account fees, and purchase fees;

that is not included in the annual operating expenses of the investment contract, product, or entity;

2. A description of the annual operating expenses (e.g., expense ratio) if the return is not fixed and any ongoing expenses in addition to annual operating expenses (e.g., wrap fees, mortality and expense fees), or, for an investment contract, product, or entity that is a designated investment alternative, the total annual operating expenses expressed as a percentage and calculated in accordance with the participant disclosure regulations at 29 CFR 2550.404a-5.

3. For an investment contract, product, or entity that is a designated investment alternative, any other information or data about the designated investment alternative that is within the control of, or reasonably available to, the CSP and that is required for the plan administrator to comply with the participant disclosure regulations at 29 CFR 2550.404a-5.

- **Investment disclosure—recordkeeping and brokerage services:** A CSP may comply with the investment disclosure section of the regulation by providing current disclosure materials of the issuer of the designated investment alternative, or information replicated from such materials, provided that the issuer
  1. is not an affiliate.
  2. is a registered investment company (mutual fund), an insurance company qualified to do business in any state, an issuer of a publicly traded security, or a financial institution supervised by a state or federal agency.
  3. the CSP acts in good faith and does not know that the materials are incomplete or inaccurate, and furnishes the responsible plan fiduciary with a statement that the CSP is making no representations as to the completeness or accuracy of the materials.

- **Manner of receipt:** A description of the manner in which the compensation will be received, such as whether the plan will be billed or the compensation will be deducted directly from the plan's accounts or investments.

Banks must update their 408(b)(2) disclosures as soon as possible but no later than 60 days following any changes to the information. Changes to investment-related compensation, however, are required to be updated only annually.

Banks may use electronic means to disclose information under the 408(b)(2) regulation to plan fiduciaries, as long as the banks' disclosures on a Web site or other electronic medium are readily accessible to plan fiduciaries and the plan fiduciaries have clear notification on how to access the information.

Best practices for banks include offering plan fiduciaries a guide, summary, or similar tool to help them identify all of the disclosures required under the regulation, particularly when service arrangements and related compensation are complex and disclosure of the information is in multiple documents. EBSA includes a sample guide in an appendix to the 408(b)(2) regulation for banks to use voluntarily as a model.

The regulation includes a class exemption from the prohibited transaction provisions of ERISA for responsible plan fiduciaries that enter into service contracts without knowing that

CSPs have failed to comply with disclosure obligations. The class exemption requires that plan fiduciaries notify the DOL of disclosure failures.

### Participant Fee Disclosure Regulation

EBSA released its 404a-5 regulation (29 CFR 2550.404a-5) to help plan participants manage and invest the money they contribute to their 401(k) pension plans. The regulation ensures that plan participants receive information regarding plan and investment related fees and expenses. This regulation has an impact on service providers, such as banks. While plan administrators (or persons designated by the plan administrator to act on its behalf) are required to disclose this information to plan participants, some of the information comes from service providers, such as banks. The regulation is intended to ensure

- plan participants are given, or have access to, the information they need to make informed decisions, including information about fees and expenses.
- delivery of investment related information is in a format that enables participants to meaningfully compare the investment options under their pension plans.
- plan administrators use standard methodologies when calculating and disclosing expense and return information (to achieve uniformity across the spectrum of investments that exist among and within plans and to facilitate apples-to-apples comparisons among the plans' investment options).
- a new level of transparency for fees and expenses.

The regulation states that the investment of plan assets is a fiduciary act governed by the fiduciary standards in ERISA 404(a)(1)(A) and (B), which require plan fiduciaries to discharge their duties with respect to the plan prudently and solely in the interest of the plan's participants and beneficiaries. The regulation also states that, when a plan allocates investment responsibilities to participants or beneficiaries, the plan administrator must take steps to ensure that the participants and beneficiaries, on a regular and periodic basis, are made aware of their rights and responsibilities with respect to the investment of assets held in, or contributed to, their accounts. The plan administrator must also ensure that participants and beneficiaries are provided sufficient information regarding the plan and the plan's investment options, including fee and expense information, so they can make informed decisions with regard to the management of their individual accounts.

Compliance with the participant disclosure regulation is a requirement for plan fiduciaries to meet their obligations under ERISA 404(a). Unlike compliance with ERISA 404(c), which is optional, all individual account plans that permit participant investment discretion must provide participant level disclosures.

On May 7, 2012, EBSA issued FAB No. 2012-02, which provides 38 questions and answers on various aspects of the 404a-5 fee disclosure regulation. FAB No. 2012-02 was updated on July 30, 2012, by modifying and replacing Q&A 30 with a new Q&A 39, which discusses a plan that offers an investment platform that includes a brokerage window, self-directed brokerage account, or similar plan arrangement. The FAB states that the platform or the brokerage window is not a designated investment alternative for purposes of the 404a-5 regulation.

Under the 404a-5 regulation, plan administrators must provide to each participant or beneficiary certain types of information in certain formats. The two major types of information are plan related and investment related. They are summarized in the following section. See 29 CFR 2550.404a-5 for complete details.

## Plan Related Information

Plan related information is the first category of disclosure information under this regulation. There are three subcategories in this first category.

### General Plan Information

On or before the date on which plan participants can first direct their account investments and at least annually thereafter, plan administrators must provide the following:

- An explanation of the circumstances under which participants and beneficiaries may give investment instructions.
- An explanation of any specified limitations on investment instructions under the terms of the plan, including any restrictions on transfer to or from an investment alternative.
- A description of or reference to plan provisions relating to the exercise of voting, tender and similar rights appurtenant to an investment in an investment alternative as well as any restrictions on such rights.
- Identification of any investment alternatives under the plan.
- Identification of any designated investment managers.
- A description of any "brokerage windows," "self-directed brokerage accounts," or similar plan arrangements that enable participants and beneficiaries to select investments beyond those designated by the plan.

### Administrative Expenses Information

On or before the date on which plan participants can first direct their account investments and at least annually thereafter, plan administrators must provide the following:

- An explanation of any fees and expenses for general plan administrative services (e.g., legal, accounting, recordkeeping) which may be charged against the individual accounts of participants and beneficiaries and are not reflected in the total annual operating expenses of any designated investment alternative, as well as the basis on which such charges will be allocated (e.g., pro rata, per capita) to, or affect the balance of, each individual account.
- At least quarterly, a statement that includes the dollar amount of the administrative fees and expenses that are actually charged (whether by liquidating shares or deducting dollars) during the preceding quarter to the participant's or beneficiary's account.

- A description of the administrative services to which the charges relate (e.g., plan administration, including recordkeeping, legal, or accounting services).
- An explanation that, in addition to the disclosed administrative fees and expenses, some of the plan's administrative expenses for the preceding quarter were paid from the total annual operating expenses of one or more of the plan's designated investment alternatives (e.g., through revenue-sharing arrangements, Rule 12b-1 fees, or subtransfer agent fees).

**Individual Expenses Information**

On or before the date on which plan participants can first direct their account investments and at least annually thereafter plan administrators must provide the following:

- An explanation of any fees and expenses that may be charged against the individual account of a participant or beneficiary on an individual, rather than on a plan wide basis (e.g., fees attendant to processing plan loans or qualified domestic relations orders (QDRO), fees for investment advice, fees for brokerage windows, commissions, front-or back-end loads or sales charges, redemption fees, transfer fees and similar expenses, and optional rider charges in annuity contracts) and which are not reflected in the total annual operating expenses of any designated investment alternative.
- At least quarterly, a statement that includes the dollar amount of the individual fees and expenses that are actually charged (whether by liquidating shares or deducting dollars) during the preceding quarter to the participant's or beneficiary's account for individual services and a description of the services to which the charges relate (e.g., loan processing fee).

## Investment Related Information—Chart Format Required

Investment related information is the second category of disclosed information under this regulation. Information must be provided on or before the date when plan participants or beneficiaries can first direct their account investments and then annually thereafter. The information must be furnished in a chart or similar format designed to facilitate a comparison of the investment related information for each investment option available under the plan. The regulation includes, as an appendix, a template of a model comparative chart. Plan administrators may use the model chart to satisfy the rule's requirement that the information be in a comparative format.

The rule provides plan administrators protection from liability for the completeness and accuracy of information provided to participants, if the plan fiduciary, reasonably and in good faith, relies on information provided by a service provider.

Plan participants must receive any materials the plan receives regarding voting, tender, or similar rights after a participant has invested in a particular investment option to the extent that such rights are passed through the plan to a plan participant. Plan administrators are required to provide to plan participants upon request or when the investment related information is provided, copies of prospectuses, financial statements or reports, statements of valuation, and a list of assets held by each investment option.

The investment related category contains several subcategories of core information about each investment option under the plan.

**Identifying information:** The name of each investment and the type or category of the investment (e.g., money market fund, balanced fund (stocks and bonds), large-cap stock fund, employer stock fund, or employer securities).

**Performance data:** Specific information that includes average annual total return of an investment that does not have a fixed rate of return, for one-, five-, and 10-calendar-year periods. For investment options that have a fixed or stated rate of return, specific information includes the annual rate of return and the term of the investment.

**Benchmarks:** The name and returns of an appropriate broad-based securities market index over one-, five-, and 10-calendar-year periods (matching the performance data periods) for investment options that do not have a fixed rate of return. The benchmark cannot be administered by an affiliate of the investment issuer, its investment adviser, or a principal underwriter, unless the index is widely recognized and used. Investment options with fixed rates of return are not subject to this requirement.

**Fee and expense information:** For investments that are not fixed, the amount and a description of each shareholder-type fee and a description of any restriction or limitation that may be applicable to a purchase, transfer, or withdrawal of the investment in whole or in part. Shareholder-type fees are fees directly charged against a participant's or beneficiary's investment, such as commissions, sales loads, sales charges, deferred sales charges, redemption fees, surrender charges, exchange fees, account fees, and purchase fees, which are not included in the total annual operating expenses of the investment. In addition, the total annual operating expenses expressed as a percentage and as a dollar amount also are required.

A statement indicating that fees and expenses are only one of several factors that participants and beneficiaries should consider when making investment decisions and a statement that the cumulative effect of fees and expenses can substantially reduce the growth of a participant's or beneficiary's retirement account must also be provided to plan participants.

For investments with a fixed return, information should include a description of and the amount of any shareholder-type fees and a description of any restriction or limitation that may be applicable to a purchase, transfer, or withdrawal of the investment in whole or in part.

**Internet Web site address:** A Web site address that is sufficiently specific to provide plan participants and beneficiaries access to such information as the issuer's name, the investment's objectives and goals, principal strategies (including a general description of the types of assets held by the investment) and principal risks, portfolio turnover rate, performance data on at least a quarterly basis, and fee and expense information.

**Glossary:** A glossary of terms to help plan participants understand the investment options, or a Web site address that is sufficiently specific to provide access to such a glossary.

On July 22, 2013, EBSA issued FAB No. 2013-02 related to the required annual fee disclosure requirement in the 404a-5 regulation. Plan administrators and service providers had expressed concern with the timing requirement of the comparative investment chart, which is required to be issued to participants and beneficiaries on an annual basis. As a temporary enforcement policy, EBSA will allow the annual comparative investment chart to be issued no later than 18 months after the prior comparative chart, provided that all the conditions stated in FAB No. 2013-02 have been met. This is only a temporary enforcement position, so banks should ensure that on a periodic basis, a determination is made as to whether EBSA has changed its position on this issue.

# Investment Management

ERISA imposes specific duties and responsibilities on fiduciaries. A person does not need to be named as a fiduciary in order to be a fiduciary. Actions are the determining factors in determining fiduciary status. When banks provide investment management services to retirement plans, they are fiduciaries and must comply with ERISA's investment standards. For all retirement plans, including those not subject to ERISA, banks must comply with 12 CFR 9 for national banks and 12 CFR 150 for federal savings associations, and other applicable laws and regulations.

Banks that act as investment managers for retirement plans should assess the needs of the plans, develop appropriate investment policies, and monitor implementation of the investment policies. For more information, refer to the "Investment Management Services" booklet of the *Comptroller's Handbook*.

The following sections address investments and related topics that present unique risks.

## Employer Securities

In terms of regulatory compliance, one of the more complex areas of plan investments involves employer securities and employer real property. Such investments are subject to various restrictions, including restrictions on the type of employer securities or employer real property, the type of plan that may hold the investments, and the percentage of plan assets invested in employer securities and employer real property.

ERISA 406(a)(1)(E) prohibits the acquisition, on behalf of a plan, of employer securities or employer real property in violation of ERISA 407(a). ERISA 407, among other things, allows such acquisitions between a plan and a party in interest, if the employer securities or employer real property are "qualifying employer securities" (QES) or "qualifying employer real property" (QERP). These terms are defined in ERISA 407(d)(4) and (5). The employer securities or employer real property must first meet the conditions in the definitions before it can be considered QES or QERP. There are implementing regulations at 29 CFR 2550.407a-1.

ERISA 407(a)(2) states that plans other than "eligible individual account plans" may not acquire QES or QERP if, immediately after such an acquisition, the aggregate fair market value of the QES or QERP held by the plan exceeds 10 percent of the fair market value of the plan's assets. This 10 percent restriction on investments in employer securities does not apply to ESOPs. See 29 CFR 2550.407a-2.

If the employee benefit plan that is acquiring the QES is not an eligible individual account plan as defined in ERISA 407(d)(3), the stock also must meet the following two requirements immediately after its acquisition by the plan in order to be a QES (ERISA 407(f)(1)):

- Not more than 25 percent of the aggregate amount of the same class of stock issued and outstanding is held by the plan.
- Persons independent of the issuer hold at least 50 percent of the aggregate amount of the same class of stock issued and outstanding.

See 29 CFR 2550.407d-5 for other QES conditions.

Under ERISA 408(e), the prohibited transaction rules regarding employer securities in ERISA 406(a)(1)(E) and 407(a) do not apply to the acquisition, sale, or lease of QES if certain conditions are met. For example, the acquisition, sale, or lease must be for adequate consideration, no commission may be charged, and the plan must be an eligible individual account plan.

Plan fiduciaries that choose to invest plan assets in their own securities must understand the potential for a conflict of interest is increased and must consider ERISA's prudence and diversification provisions. While a plan may be able to acquire employer securities or real property under the employer securities rules, the acquisition must be for the exclusive benefit of participants and beneficiaries.

Some plan sponsors are uncomfortable with even having employer stock as an investment option in a participant-directed plan. These plan sponsors may eliminate company stock from a 401(k) menu or prohibit new investments in a company stock fund within the plan. Other plan sponsors are setting a maximum allocation that participants can have to employer stock or offering extensive communications/education on the value of diversification and the risk of large concentrations in a single investment.

Even when the retirement plan is a participant-directed individual account plan, recent litigation has generated concerns that fiduciaries might have an obligation to disregard participant directions to invest in QES in certain situations. For many years, courts have followed the *Moench* presumption of prudence. The *Moench* presumption was established by a 1995 decision by the Third Circuit Court of Appeals. (*Moench v. Robertson,* 62 F3d 553, 3d Cir. 1995). The Third Circuit addressed the question of the extent to which fiduciaries of ESOPs may be held liable under ERISA for investing solely in employer common stock when the terms of the ESOP provide that the primary purpose of the plan is to invest in the employer's securities. The court concluded that in limited circumstances, ESOP fiduciaries can be held liable under ERISA for continuing to invest in employer stock. The court continued by stating that an ESOP fiduciary that invests in employer stock in accordance with the terms of the plan is entitled to a presumption that it acted consistently with ERISA. That presumption may be overcome, however, if it can be shown that the fiduciary abused its discretion. Abuse of discretion may be proven when ESOP fiduciaries are also directors of the corporation and the financial state of the company deteriorates. The prudent man standard in ERISA requires that fiduciaries with dual loyalties must make a careful and impartial investigation of all investment decisions.

There are significant differences among federal circuit courts regarding the application of *Moench.* While many circuit courts, including the Second, Third, Fifth, Sixth, Ninth and 11th Circuits, have expressly adopted the *Moench* presumption, not all courts have yet done so. Even among those that have, significant differences remain as to its application and its scope.[3] The issue may soon be settled as the Supreme Court granted certiorari to petitioners in *Fifth Third Bancorp v. Dudenhoeffer* (692 F.3d 410 (6th Cir. 2012)) to settle the circuit split over whether and at what stage in the litigation fiduciaries that continue to offer employer stock as an investment option in a 401(k)-style plan as the stock price declines are presumed to have acted prudently.[4] Plan fiduciaries making decisions regarding investment in employer stock should monitor this area of the law for developments concerning the scope of their fiduciary obligations.

Banks acting as trustee generally do not invest retirement plan assets in employer securities or employer real property, unless properly directed. Although such an investment may be permissible, banks should use reasonable risk management processes and enlist the aid of legal counsel when appropriate, to determine whether the transaction meets the appropriate ERISA prohibited transaction exemptions. For more information, see the "Fiduciary Responsibilities of Directed Trustees" section of this booklet.

## Mutual Funds

Banks should have a sound mutual fund selection process when putting together menus of investment options for participant-directed plans and for plan investments when banks serve as investment managers.

Even though several courts have stated in their written decisions that when banks decide which mutual funds to include on the banks' menus of investment options and which share

---

[3] In *Taveras v. UBS Ag,* No. 12-1662-cv (2d Cir. Feb. 27, 2013), the Second Circuit held that ERISA plan fiduciaries are not entitled to a presumption that they acted prudently by offering plan participants the opportunity to invest in employer stock where the plan's terms merely permit—but do not in the court's view require or "strongly encourage"—employer stock as a plan investment option. In *Harris v. Amgen Inc.,* No. 10-56014 (9th Cir. June 4, 2013), the Ninth Circuit Court of Appeals ruled that ERISA plan fiduciaries were not entitled to a rebuttable presumption that their decision to continue to offer an employer stock fund as a retirement plan option satisfied ERISA's duty of prudence, even though such a fund was expressly contemplated by the plan documents. The Ninth Circuit concluded that the *Moench* presumption did not apply in cases where the terms of the plan did not "require or encourage" that an employer stock fund be offered as an investment option.

[4] Cert. granted, No. 12-751 (U.S. Dec. 13, 2013).

---

classes of those funds will be offered is not a fiduciary decision but rather a product-design decision,[5] the OCC expects banks to implement a well-documented, disciplined selection and monitoring process that includes adopting and following written policies and procedures. Banks should be alert to potential prohibited transactions when using proprietary mutual funds. The use of proprietary funds when the bank has discretion may trigger a conflict of interest. For more information, see the "Conflicts of Interest" booklet of the *Comptroller's Handbook*.

The use of proprietary funds for the bank's own employee benefit plan may also trigger litigation against the bank. Several lawsuits have been brought by participants against plan sponsors that are banks. The complaints have alleged that the bank violated its fiduciary duties by selecting proprietary mutual funds as investment options in participant-directed 401(k) plans.[6] Banks that offer proprietary funds for its own employee benefit plan should make sure all the conditions of PTE 77-3 are being met.

## Stable Value Funds

Stable value funds are capital preservation investment options available in many 401(k) plans and other types of pension plans. The funds are invested in a high-quality, diversified fixed-income portfolio that is protected against interest rate volatility by contracts (wraps) from banks and insurance companies. Stable value funds are designed to preserve capital while providing steady, positive returns. Stable value funds are considered a conservative and low-risk investment, but they can be very different depending on the underlying portfolio and the contract (wrap) offered by the insurance company or bank. It is important for banks to completely understand the stable value funds that they are offering to plan fiduciaries, and it is critical that banks provide plan fiduciaries complete and transparent information regarding the stable value funds.

Stable value funds are structured as either a separately managed account, which is a stable value fund managed for one specific 401(k) plan, or a commingled fund, which pools together assets from many 401(k) plans.

Regardless of how stable funds are structured, they comprise a diversified portfolio of fixed-income securities that are insulated from interest rate movements by contracts (wraps) from banks and insurance companies. The protection from interest rate volatility is universal to stable value funds. How this contract protection is delivered depends on the type of stable

---

[5] *Leimkuehler v. American United Life Insurance Co.*, Nos. 12-1081, 12-1213 & 12-2536 (7th Cir. April 16, 2013). *Hecker v. Deere & Co.*, 556 F.3d 575 (7th Cir. 2009).

[6] *David v. Alphin*, No. 11-2181 (4th Cir. Jan. 14, 2013)—upheld dismissal with prejudice. *Krueger v. Ameriprise Financial, Inc.*, No. 11-CV-02781 (2012 U.S. Dist. Lexis 166191, November 20, 2012). *Gipson v. Wells Fargo*, No. 08-4546 (2010 U.S. Dist. Lexis 79965, April 6, 2010). *Leber v. CitiGroup, Inc.*, No. 07-CiV-9329 (2011 U.S. District Lexis 129444, November 8, 2011). *Franklin v. First Union Corp.*, No. 3:99CV344, 84 F.Supp.2d 720, February 17, 2000. *Figas v. Wells Fargo & Co.*, No. 08-4546 (2010 U.S. Dist. Lexis 79965, April 6, 2010).

value fund investment. The contract protection against interest rate volatility is offered through the following investment instruments:

- **A guaranteed investment contract.** A guaranteed investment contract is a contract with an insurance company that provides principal preservation and a specified rate of return over a set period of time, regardless of the performance of the underlying invested assets. The invested assets are owned by the insurance company and held within the insurer's general account.
- **A separate account contract.** A separate account contract is an account held by an insurance company that holds a combination of fixed-income securities and provides principal preservation and a specified rate of return over a set period of time. Separate accounts may provide either a fixed rate of return or a periodic rate of return based on the performance of the underlying assets. The assets are owned by the insurance company and are set aside in a separate account solely for the benefit of the specific contract holder.
- **A synthetic guaranteed investment contract.** A synthetic guaranteed investment contract is a diversified portfolio of fixed-income securities that are insulated from interest rate volatility by contracts (wraps) from banks and insurance companies. In this arrangement, the 401(k) plan and its participants own the underlying invested assets (the portfolio of fixed-income securities that supports the stable value fund.)

The typical stable value fund diversifies contract protection by investing in more than one instrument type or with more than one insurance company or bank.

The market value of all fixed-income investments, including the underlying assets in a stable value fund, is volatile by nature. As interest rates move up, the market value of the assets declines, and vice versa. Unlike other 401(k) investments, all stable value funds have protection against interest rate swings by way of protections made possible through insurance company and bank contracts (wraps). This means investors in stable value funds are able to transact (make deposits, withdrawals, transfers, etc.) at book or contract value. This is principal plus accrued interest. Should the market value of the stable value fund's underlying assets be insufficient to honor benefits for covered withdrawals at book value, the contractual protection (wrap) kicks in to ensure that participants continue to transact at contract value. Contract value, or book value, is the value of all assets supporting the stable value fund plus the contractual protection against interest rate volatility.

There are a few, limited instances when participants do not get book value from a stable value fund. These limited instances are typically defined in the contract. One such instance typically not covered is security defaults or downgrades. To protect the integrity of the stable value fund, most contracts incorporate investment guidelines establishing minimum credit quality requirements for the underlying securities. These contracts have established mechanisms to address downgraded or defaulted securities that fall outside the contractual guidelines. Corporate-initiated events—which are employer-driven events, such as an early retirement program, layoff, or bankruptcy—are also typically not covered. Corporate-initiated events generally cause withdrawals en masse from a stable value fund. These withdrawals can negatively impact investors and plans that choose to remain in the fund.

Stable value funds do not have waiting periods or surrender charges for participants. Most stable value funds have equity wash provisions that restrict transfers from stable value funds directly to competing funds. Competing funds are typically money market funds or short-duration bond funds. The restriction requires transfers from the stable value fund to sit in an equity fund for a set period of time, usually 90 days before the transfer is invested in a competing fund. In cases where a plan sponsor wishes to terminate its participation in a commingled stable value fund, a 12-month or longer put or waiting period may be imposed to protect the remaining investors by ensuring an orderly liquidation of the departing fund's proportionate share of the stable value fund's underlying assets. Plan participants continue to transact at book/contract value. Given its fixed nature, guaranteed investment contracts may impose a surrender charge if the stable value fund elects to terminate the contract before its stated maturity date.

## Self-Directed Brokerage

More and more frequently, self-directed brokerage accounts are being offered as an investment alternative for 401(k) and other pension plans. Generally, self-directed brokerage accounts offer plan participants the opportunity to invest among a broad array of investment vehicles, which are in addition to the "core" investment options selected by the plan fiduciary.

There are several types of self-directed brokerage accounts.

- **Mutual fund window:** A mutual fund window allows participants to invest among a universe of mutual funds. The plan fiduciary selects the universe. The universe may be limited to as few as 20 mutual funds or the universe may be open to any mutual fund that the bank, as a service provider, offers to any of its employee benefit plan clients.
- **Brokerage accounts:** Brokerage accounts may be established for each participant with a registered broker-dealer to implement the self-directed brokerage option under a plan. In that event, any investment sold by the broker is available to the participants unless the plan fiduciary limits the range of investments that participants can select. Many plans impose a variety of limits on the investments available through a self-directed brokerage account.

Self-directed brokerage accounts appeal to participants that want access to securities or funds outside the plan's core investment options. Establishing a self-directed brokerage account may be a better option for a plan fiduciary that has such participants rather than adding more securities or funds to the plan's core investment options. Many active traders want access to a self-directed brokerage account in their participant-directed 401(k) plan so that they may actively trade on a tax-advantaged basis. The downside to a self-directed brokerage account is that participants may incur higher costs, including commissions, transaction fees, and account maintenance fees. In addition, participants may be required to pay "retail" for any mutual fund that is not a "core" plan option, which means participants may be subject to front-end loads or mutual fund shares with higher fees. Unsophisticated participants may incur investment losses as well as increased trading costs.

Plans also have some disadvantages when establishing a self-directed brokerage account. By adding a self-directed brokerage account or mutual fund window, the plan may incur higher service costs. This is because the establishment of an interface between the plan's recordkeeper and the broker-dealer for the self-directed brokerage account could increase plan administrative expenses. Additional expenses may be incurred in connection with plan auditing and valuation as well as participant communication material.

The plan fiduciary responsible for establishing a plan's self-directed brokerage account arrangement or mutual fund window must prudently select and monitor the arrangement and provider. The broker-dealer's service capability and capacity should be carefully reviewed, such as previous experience with ERISA plans; investment information, education, and advice services; and the capability to impose and monitor procedural limits on participant trades imposed under the plan. The plan fiduciary should also consider (among other things) fee arrangements, protection for errors, reporting and disclosure to the plan fiduciary and to participants, custody and control of the plan's assets, and provisions for terminating the service relationship.

The plan fiduciary must document that any limits on participation in the self-directed brokerage account window is justified as reasonable. Many plans require participants to transfer at least a minimum amount to a self-directed brokerage account or attempt to limit use of the self-directed brokerage account to no more than 50 percent of the participant's account balance at the time of a transfer to the self-directed brokerage account. Periodic testing may be required to ensure that the eligible group is non-discriminatory under IRC rules.

EBSA has issued guidance relating to self-directed brokerage accounts in connection with the 404a-5 participant disclosure regulations. FAB No. 2012-02 was issued on May 7, 2012. It provides 38 questions and answers on various aspects of the 404a-5 fee disclosure regulation. FAB No. 2012-02 was updated on July 30, 2012, by modifying and replacing Q&A 30 with a new Q&A 39, which discusses a plan that offers an investment platform that includes a brokerage window, self-directed brokerage account, or similar plan arrangement. The FAB states that the platform or the brokerage window is not a designated investment alternative for purposes of the 404a-5 regulation. For more information, please see the fee disclosures section of this handbook.

## Bank or Holding Company Securities

There may be occasions when a bank serves as a directed trustee to a defined contribution plan and is directed to purchase shares of its own bank stock or the stock of its holding company parent. AO 92-23A addresses this situation, and the DOL states that there would be no prohibited transaction violations under ERISA 406(a) or (b) if certain conditions are met. The DOL, in coming to this conclusion, refers to the Conference Report that accompanied ERISA upon passage into law in 1974. The Conference Report states: "In general, it is expected that a transaction will not be a prohibited transaction if the transaction is an ordinary "blind" transaction purchase or sale of securities through an exchange where neither the buyer or seller (nor the agent of either) knows the identity of the other party involved."

The conditions that would lead to a conclusion of no prohibited transaction violations in this situation are

- if such stock purchases are made on the open market.
- through an unaffiliated broker-dealer.
- no more than fair market value is paid for the stock.
- the bank receives no commission as a result of the purchase.
- the direction is from a named fiduciary having the authority to direct investments or from an investment manager appointed by a named fiduciary.

## Asset Concentrations

ERISA 404(a)(1)(C) states that a plan fiduciary must act solely in the interest of the plan's participants and beneficiaries and diversify the investments of the plan so as to minimize the risk of large losses, unless under the circumstances it is clearly prudent not to do so.

If a bank has investment discretion, it should have processes in place to monitor concentrations and should maintain documentation to demonstrate the prudence of specific asset concentrations.

## Definition of Plan Assets in Connection With Plan Investments

The general rule, under 29 CFR 2510.3.101(a)(2), is that when a plan invests in an investment vehicle, the plan's assets include its investment, but do not, solely by reason of the investment, include any of the underlying assets of the investment vehicle. The general rule applies to such investment vehicles as publicly offered securities, mutual funds, operating companies (defined in regulation, see summary below), and where "the percentage of employee benefit investors in the investment vehicle is not significant" (defined in regulation, see summary below). An example would be a plan that is invested in a mutual fund. The plan owns shares in the mutual fund but not any of the underlying assets that make up the mutual fund.

An exception to the general rule for certain types of plan investment vehicles, known as the "look-through" rule, provides that in the case of a plan's investment in an equity interest in certain investment vehicles, the plan's assets include both the equity interest and an undivided interest in each of the underlying assets of the investment vehicle. An example would be a plan that is invested in a bank collective investment fund. The plan owns units of the collective investment fund as well as the underlying assets of the bank collective investment fund.

The importance of knowing if the general rule applies or the look-through rule applies to a plan investment vehicle is if a bank exercises authority or control respecting the management or disposition of the underlying assets of the investment vehicle or the bank provides investment advice for a fee (directly or indirect) to the investment vehicle, the bank automatically becomes a fiduciary of the plan that is invested in the investment vehicle. For example, if a plan is invested in a bank collective investment fund and the bank is not a trustee to the plan nor does it have investment discretion, it is still a fiduciary to the plan because of the look-through rule.

As previously described, the general rule and not the look-through rule applies where the investment vehicle is an operating company and where the percentage of employee benefit investors in the investment vehicle is not significant. An operating company is an entity that is primarily engaged in the production or sale of a product or service other than the investment of capital (29 CFR 2510.3-101(c)). The term includes "venture capital operating companies" and "real estate operating companies" (29 CFR 2510.3-101(d) and (e)).

Many hedge funds and private equity funds want to come under the general rule and rely on "the percentage of employee benefit investors in the investment vehicle is not significant" test (29 CFR 2510.3-101(f)). Under this section of the regulation, equity participation in an investment vehicle by employee benefit plan investors is significant on any date if, immediately after the most recent acquisition of any equity interest in the investment vehicle, 25 percent or more of the value of any class of equity interest in the investment vehicle is held by benefit plan investors (as defined in the regulation). If the hedge funds and private equity funds meet the "percentage of employee benefit investors in the investment vehicle is not significant" test, then assets of the fund are not plan assets under ERISA and the investment manager of the fund is not an ERISA fiduciary.

What makes it somewhat easier for hedge funds, private equity funds, and similar vehicles to meet the "percentage of employee benefit investors in the investment vehicle is not significant" test is the definition of benefit plan investors in the regulation at 29 CFR 2510.3-101(f)(2). The term "benefit plan investor" no longer includes public plans, non-U.S. plans, and other plans not subject to ERISA. Funds investing in the investment vehicle are only counted as benefit plan investors to the extent of the percentage interest in the investment vehicle held by benefit plan investors.

## Alternative Investments and Unique Assets

Banks that have investment discretion over employee benefit plan assets have a duty to prudently manage assets, including alternative, nonmarketable, or unique assets, such as hedge funds, real estate, derivatives, and personal notes. Banks should have policies and procedures that establish whether a particular investment furthers the purposes of the plan, taking into consideration

- liquidity needs of the plan.
- availability of valuation information and marketability of the asset.
- experience of the bank (or of the expert hired by the bank to manage the asset).
- plan's other investments.
- plan's investment strategy.
- loss that a divestiture would cause to the plan.

Banks are not required to be experts in all the investments of a plan's assets. As fiduciaries, however, banks are required to seek the advice or retain the services of an expert when dealing with investments in which they do not have expertise or when conducting reviews of an investment adviser that is outside their area of expertise.

For further information, banks should refer to the "Unique and Hard-to-Value Assets" booklet of the *Comptroller's Handbook*.

## Cross-Trades

Banks, in their capacity as investment managers, may cross-trade securities between accounts they manage. Cross-trades involve purchases of securities from a pension plan account to the sale of those same securities to another account managed by the bank (and vice versa). There is a statutory exemption for the cross-trading of securities; the exemption is found at ERISA 408(b)(19), and the implementing regulation is at 29 CFR 2550.408b-19, which provides a prohibited transaction exemption for cross-trades. The exemption is for both ERISA 406(a) and (b) violations. There is a parallel exemption at IRC 4975(d)(22).

Banks with investment discretion that wish to cross-trade securities of retirement plans need to establish appropriate controls to meet all the conditions contained in the statutory exemption and implementing regulation.

The statutory exemption extends only to plans (or master trusts containing the assets of plans maintained by employers in the same controlled group) that have assets of at least $100 million. Other conditions are summarized as follows (see statute and regulation for complete details).

- The transaction is a purchase or sale, for no consideration other than cash payment against prompt delivery of a security for which market quotations are readily available.
- The transaction is effected at the independent, current market price of the security.
- No brokerage commission fee (except for customary transfer fees, the fact of which is disclosed) or other remuneration is paid in connection with the transaction.
- A fiduciary (other than the bank as investment manager engaging in the cross-trades or any affiliate) for each plan participating in the transaction authorizes in advance of any cross-trades the bank as investment manager to engage in cross-trades at the bank's discretion, after the fiduciary has received disclosure regarding the conditions under which cross-trades may take place including the written policies and procedures of the bank. The disclosure must be separate from any other agreement or disclosure involving the asset management relationship.
- The bank as investment manager provides to the plan fiduciary, who authorized the cross-trading, a quarterly report detailing all cross-trades executed by the bank in which the plan participated during such quarter, including the following information, as applicable:
  - Identity of each security bought or sold.
  - Number of shares or units traded.
  - Parties involved in the cross-trade.
  - Trade price and the method used to establish the trade price.
- The bank as investment manager does not base its fee schedule on the plan's consent to cross-trading, and no other service (other than the investment opportunities and cost

savings available through a cross-trade) is conditioned on the plan's consent to cross trading.

- The bank as investment manager has adopted, and cross-trades are effected in accordance with, written cross-trading policies and procedures that are fair and equitable to all accounts participating in the cross-trading program. The cross-trading policies and procedures include a description of the manager's pricing policies and procedures and methods of allocating cross-trades in an objective manner among accounts participating in the cross-trading program.

- The bank as investment manager has designated an individual responsible for periodically reviewing such purchases and sales to ensure compliance with the written cross-trading policies and procedures. Following such review, the individual shall issue an annual written report no later than 90 days following the period to which it relates, signed under penalty of perjury, to the plan fiduciary that authorized the cross-trading. The report describes the steps performed during the course of the review, level of compliance, and any specific instances of noncompliance. The written report shall also notify the plan fiduciary of the plan's right to terminate participation in the bank's cross-trading program at any time.

There is a PTE 2002-12 that permits certain cross-trades of securities among index- and model-driven funds. The exemption affects EB plans invested in index- or model-driven funds and large pension plans and other large accounts involved in portfolio restructuring programs.

The exemption provides relief from the restrictions in ERISA (406(a)(1)(A) and 406(b)(2)) for

- the purchase and sale of securities between an index- or model-driven fund and another such fund, at least one of which holds "plan assets" subject to ERISA.
- the purchase and sale of securities between index- or model-driven funds and certain large accounts, at least one of which holds "plan assets" subject to ERISA, pursuant to a portfolio restructuring program of the large accounts.
- cross-trades between two or more large accounts pursuant to a portfolio restructuring program if such cross-trades occur as part of a single cross-trading program involving both index- or model-driven funds and large accounts for which securities are cross-traded solely as a result of the objective operation of the program.

PTE 2002-12 contains a number of conditions. For example, any cross-trade of securities by an index- or model-driven fund must occur as a direct result of a "triggering event" and executed no later than close of business the third business day after the triggering event. Another example is, if the cross-trade involves a model-driven fund, the cross-trade must not take place within three business days after any change made by the manager to the model underlying the model-driven fund. See PTE 2002-12 for all the conditions of the exemption.

## Derivatives

On March 21, 1996, the DOL published an Information Letter addressed to OCC Comptroller Eugene Ludwig regarding the investment of ERISA plan assets in derivatives (the Ludwig Letter). In the Ludwig Letter, the DOL confirmed that investments in derivatives are subject to the fiduciary standards applicable to other plan investments. Accordingly, plan fiduciaries considering an investment in derivatives are required to engage in the same general procedures and make the same type of analysis that they would in making any other investment decision. This would include a consideration of how the investment fits within the plan's investment policy, what role the particular derivative plays in the plan's portfolio, and the plan's potential exposure to losses. As with any investment made by a plan, plan fiduciaries with the authority to invest in derivatives are responsible for securing sufficient information to understand a particular investment before making it. For example, plan fiduciaries should secure from dealers and other sellers of derivatives, among other things, sufficient information to allow an independent analysis of the credit risk and market risk undertaken by the plan in making the investment in the particular derivative. The market risks presented by the derivatives purchased by the plan should be understood and evaluated in terms of the effects that they have on the relevant segments of the plan's portfolio as well as the portfolio's overall risk. Plan fiduciaries should also understand and evaluate the operational and legal risks presented by the derivatives.

The Ludwig Letter emphasizes that while derivatives may be a useful tool for managing a variety of risks and for broadening investment alternatives in a plan's portfolio, investments in certain derivatives, such as structured notes and collateralized mortgage obligations, may require a higher degree of sophistication and understanding on the part of plan fiduciaries than other investments. Characteristics of such derivatives may include extreme price volatility, a high degree of leverage, limited testing by markets, and difficulty in determining the market value of the derivative due to illiquid market conditions.

Over the years since the enactment of ERISA, plan fiduciaries have frequently engaged in derivatives contract trading, especially with regard to financial futures as a hedging tool in order to minimize risks associated with fluctuating interest rates.

In AO 82-49A, the DOL provided guidance to ERISA plans engaging in futures transactions on a contract market through futures commission merchants (FCM).

Futures trading involves the buying and selling of the rights and obligations attendant upon making or taking delivery of a commodity at some date in the future. Plan fiduciaries that want to trade in futures contracts place an order with an FCM. The FCM acts as an agent for the customer and transmits the customer's order to a broker who executes the order on a designated contract market. When a customer engages in a futures transaction through an FCM, the customer is required to pay to the FCM an amount equal to a small percentage of the contract amount called initial margin. The FCM may require a higher amount of initial margin based on the creditworthiness of each customer or other relevant characteristics. Subsequent payments, called maintenance or variation margin, to or from the FCM may be required as the price of the underlying commodity fluctuates, making the long and short positions in the futures contract more or less valuable.

In AO 82-49A, the DOL stated that the assets held by the FCM to fund a plan's margin account (consisting of initial and maintenance margin in connection with a future transaction) are not plan assets. Instead, when a plan engages in a futures transaction, the plan assets are the rights to payment from the margin account under certain circumstances as embodied in the futures contract and the agreement with the FCM. The DOL also stated that an FCM is not acting as a plan fiduciary when executing a sale or purchase of futures on behalf of the plan pursuant to instructions from the plan fiduciary. Rather, the FCM acts as an agent of the plan fiduciary. The FCM is also not a fiduciary during the liquidation of plan futures accounts if the agreement between the FCM and the plan fiduciary provides details as to the FCM's actions if the plan fiduciary does not meet a maintenance margin call and the FCM closes out the plan's account.

The DOL has taken a similar position with regard to cleared swap transactions. The Dodd–Frank Wall Street Reform and Consumer Protection Act (Dodd–Frank) and U.S. Commodity Futures Trading Commission (CFTC) regulations require the clearing of certain standardized derivative products such as swaps. A swap is defined to include any bilateral agreement in which counterparties exchange cash flows of one party's financial instrument for those of the other party's financial instrument at specified intervals based on a notional principal amount. Retirement plans are regular users of swap contracts.

It is a violation of the Commodity Exchange Act for any person to engage in a swap that is required to be cleared without submitting the swap for clearing through a designated clearing organization (DCO), also known as a central counterparty or clearinghouse, absent an available exemption. Swaps are submitted for clearing with the DCO on behalf of a plan fiduciary through its FCM, which is a "clearing member" (CM) of that DCO (or has a relationship with a second FCM that is a CM of the DCO). Plan fiduciaries are required to post initial margin with the DCO and daily variation margin, as required.

On February 7, 2013, the DOL issued AO 2013-01A in response to an industry request seeking clarity regarding the application of ERISA to certain cleared swap transactions. The DOL in AO 2013-01A stated that margin held by the CM in connection with a swap transaction is not a plan asset. The plan assets are the rights embodied in the swap contract as evidenced by the written agreement between the plan and the CM. The DOL also stated that neither the DCO nor a CM is a fiduciary in the event the plan fails to meet a margin call or other contractually specified default event. AO 2013-01A clarifies that a DCO's provision of clearing services for the plan's CM does not cause it to be deemed a party in interest with respect to the plan. The CM, however, is considered to be a party in interest to the plan due, among other things, to the direct contractual agreement with the plan and procurement of clearing and other services. Because the CM is considered to be a party in interest, certain transactions between the plan and the CM that occur in connection with swap transactions are prohibited under section 406(a) of ERISA unless an exemption applies. PTE 84-14 (the Qualified Professional Asset Manager Exemption) provides relief in this situation provided all the conditions of the exemption are met.

CFTC rules implementing Dodd–Frank's business conduct requirements for swap dealers (SD) and major swap participants (MSP) in their dealings with counterparties including "special entities"—a term that includes employee benefit plans defined under ERISA—are found in 17 CFR 23.400 et seq. Pursuant to the Commodity Futures Trading Commission rules, an SD/MSP that offers to enter or enters into a swap with an ERISA plan must have "a reasonable basis to believe" that the plan has a representative that is an ERISA fiduciary. The rules provide for a safe harbor whereby an SD/MSP is deemed to have a "reasonable basis to believe" that a plan has an ERISA fiduciary if the plan provides the fiduciary's name and contact information and represents that the representative is a fiduciary as defined in section 3 of ERISA. With respect to an ERISA plan, an SD does not act as an advisor to the plan if the plan represents in writing that (1) it has an ERISA fiduciary; (2) the fiduciary represents in writing that it will not rely on the SD's recommendations; and (3) it will comply in good faith with written policies and procedures reasonably designed to ensure that any recommendation it receives from the SD materially affecting a swap transaction is evaluated by a fiduciary before the transaction occurs.

## Hedge Funds and Private Equity Investing

Plan fiduciaries are increasingly investing defined benefit plan assets in a wide range of investments, including hedge funds and private equity funds (either directly or through a fund of funds). Some of the reasons for this include

- the need to increase diversification of plan assets.
- an attempt to decrease the volatility within the plan that has been, in recent years, associated with traditional investments in stocks and bonds.
- an effort to enhance the plan's overall investment performance.

Participant-directed, defined contribution plans may also have exposure to hedge funds or private equity funds when the plan includes as part of its investment options target-date funds, life cycle funds, or other funds that may invest a portion of the fund's assets in hedge funds or private equity funds. Banks, in choosing investment vehicles to place on their participant-directed, defined contribution menus or platforms, or as investment managers or advisers to defined benefit plans, may be involved in these types of investments.

The DOL does not impose quantitative limits on a plan's investment in these investments but rather evaluates the appropriateness of the investment under ERISA's general fiduciary and prudence standards. In addition, the DOL has confirmed that the analysis in the Ludwig letter, with regard to derivatives, is applicable to pension plans investing in hedge funds or private equity funds.

The term hedge fund is widely used and generally refers to a diverse group of funds not registered with the SEC. Hedge funds invest in different types of assets, e.g., long or short positions in exchange-traded securities, exchange-traded and off-exchange derivatives, currencies, commodities, and different types of investment products. They often use relatively high levels of leverage. Private equity funds are pooled investment vehicles that typically make investments in companies that do not have publicly traded equity.

In a "fund of funds" arrangement, plans can have exposure to private equity or hedge fund investments by investing in a fund that invests in several private equity or hedge funds. This type of investing provides a benefit as it provides access to funds that are not normally available to a plan. This investment option also increases diversification of the pension plan's portfolio and shifts some of the due diligence function, as well as ongoing oversight of the investment, to the investment professionals associated with the fund. It is important to note that there are also certain disadvantages associated with this investment approach, including increased fees and costs at the fund of funds level and less transparency of the underlying funds and investment components.

Although investing in hedge funds or private equity funds may offer increased opportunities for gain, these funds present inherent risks and complexities. Some important points of concern regarding these types of investments include the following:

- **Liquidity:** They are less liquid than traditional investments.
- **Valuation:** It may be difficult to determine the current value of the funds.
- **Transparency:** It may be difficult to get details regarding investment holdings, degree of leverage being used, or overall investment strategy.
- **Investment strategy:** Investment strategies may greatly vary over time, making past performance irrelevant.

Banks need to have policies in place relative to the prudent selection and monitoring of these alternative investment options. The policies should address the following:

- **Appropriateness of investing in hedge funds and private equity funds.**
- **Evaluating past performance:** Changing fund strategies can lead to large variations in fund performance. Index construction to evaluate performance is especially difficult for hedge funds because of the variety of different hedge fund strategies and the substantial rate of turnover among funds. Because private equity funds are generally closed-end, finite horizon funds, they have no track record.
- **Evaluating fees:** Investments in both hedge funds and private equity funds generally have substantial fees. These fees usually include a management fee charged as a percentage of assets under management and may include a performance fee. There may be additional fees for placement, early redemption of the investment, and for administration. There may also be provisions for "claw backs" in which fees already paid to management may be partly refunded to investors if multi-year, contractual benchmarks are not reached.
- **Evaluating liquidity:** Investments in hedge funds, especially private equity funds, are relatively illiquid. For private equity funds there is often a capital commitment period of three to five years, with the possibility of a 10-year lock-up period. Given this illiquidity, it is critical that the overall liquidity structure of the investment portfolio matches the need to pay out benefits under the plan.
- **Issues relating to monitoring and due diligence:** Banks should determine whether they have the necessary time and expertise associated with the selection and ongoing monitoring of these investment options. If hiring an investment adviser who has expertise

in evaluating and monitoring these types of investments, banks should understand how the adviser performs the required risk analysis and due diligence.

## Target Date Funds or Life Cycle Funds

Target date or life cycle funds are increasingly popular investment alternatives in participant-directed retirement plans such as 401(k) plans. Target date retirement funds make investing for retirement more convenient by automatically changing the fund's allocation among asset classes, such as stocks, bonds, and cash, over time. Such funds typically become more conservative as the retirement date nears, but under some structures the funds only start to become more conservative after the designated retirement date.

The losses suffered by target date funds in the midst of the market crisis in late 2008 and early 2009 raised concerns about the design and transparency of these funds. The date used in the name of a target date fund has not always been consistent with the design of the fund, making these funds difficult for investors to evaluate and compare. In other words, the allocation of assets among stocks, bonds, and cash-equivalents vary greatly among target date funds with the same target retirement date. For example, in a 2015 target date fund, the equity holdings can range anywhere from over 20 percent to as high as over 60 percent. Some target date funds may not reach their most conservative investment mix until 20 or 30 years after the target date. This is because some target date funds assume a full distribution at the target retirement date, often called "to" target retirement date funds, while others assume a stream of payments throughout the employees' retirement, often called "through" target retirement date funds. The time horizon and asset allocation for a target date fund "to" 2015 would be much different than for a target date fund "through" 2015. In addition, target date funds with the same target date may have different investment results and may charge different fees. Finally, the target date fund may charge a fee and the underlying mutual funds may charge a fee when target date funds invest in other mutual funds in a fund of funds arrangement.

Banks using target date or life cycle funds in their participant-directed, defined contribution menus or platforms should document that they fully understand the "glide path" of a target date fund. This is the rate at which the fund shifts its investment portfolio to reduce market risk. Banks should know that the date in the name of the target date fund is not always consistent with the design of the fund. Does the target date fund become more conservative as the retirement date nears, or is the most conservative investment mix achieved 20 or 30 years after the retirement date? All marketing, RFP material, or participant material should be accurate when describing the target date funds' investment strategies.

Banks should be cautious regarding benchmarking the return of a target date fund for monitoring purposes. Banks should examine a target date fund's stated benchmark to see if it actually represents the asset allocation of the fund. The various asset allocation strategies can flaw attempts to benchmark by retirement year.

The DOL issued "Target Date Retirement Funds - Tips for ERISA Plan Fiduciaries" in February 2013. This document contains a series of items (with significant explanation) that plan fiduciaries should consider when selecting and monitoring target date funds as an investment option in participant-directed, individual account plans. Plan fiduciaries should

- establish a process for comparing and selecting target date funds.
- establish a process for the periodic review of selected target date funds.
- understand the fund's investments—the allocation in different asset classes (stocks, bonds, cash), individual investments, and how these change over time.
- review the fund's fees and investment expenses.
- inquire whether a custom or nonproprietary target fund would be a better fit for the plan.
- develop effective employee communications.
- take advantage of available sources of information to evaluate the target date fund, and recommendations received regarding the target date fund selection.
- document the process.

# Compensation Issues

## 12b-1 and Other Fees

**<u>From proprietary mutual funds—bank has investment discretion.</u>** If a bank wants to use proprietary mutual funds, and it has investment discretion over the employee benefit fund assets, then it must meet all the provisions of prohibited transaction exemption PTE 77-4, or the bank needs to have an individual prohibited transaction exemption. Otherwise, a bank's use of investment discretion to invest retirement plan assets in shares of affiliated mutual funds constitutes a prohibited transaction. PTE 77-4 provides an exemption from the prohibited transaction restrictions under ERISA 406 and IRC 4975 for the purchase and sale by an employee benefit plan of mutual fund shares when a fiduciary with respect to the plan (bank trustee) is also the investment adviser for the mutual fund (or an affiliate of the bank is the investment adviser for the mutual fund).

Among other things, the exemption states that there cannot be any payment of sales commissions in connection with the purchase or sale of mutual fund shares. In addition, the plan may not pay "double" investment advisory, or investment management, fees with respect to the plan assets invested in the mutual fund shares. To satisfy this condition, the plan either must not pay the bank a plan level investment advisory or management fee with respect to those assets or must receive a credit against its plan level fee for its pro rata share of investment advisory fees paid by the mutual fund. There are also disclosure and consent requirements in PTE 77-4 that must be met.

The DOL in AO 93-26A discusses the use of proprietary mutual funds for IRAs and concludes that IRAs are included in the term "employee benefit plan" as used in PTE 77-4. In AO 2005-10A, the DOL addresses the question of whether the receipt of fees from proprietary funds violated IRC 4975(c)(1)(E) or (F) if a bank was acting as trustee or custodian for IRA accounts and also providing investment advice to the IRA account holder. The DOL determined that if the bank reduced its IRA management fee by an amount equal to the fees it received from the proprietary funds and the receipt of the fees from the proprietary funds did not cause the bank's compensation to exceed the amount of the IRA management

Comptroller's Handbook      46      Retirement Plan Products and Services fees, there were no prohibited transaction violations under the code. The DOL added that if the bank were to provide the same service to employee benefit plans, the same analysis and conclusions would lead the DOL to conclude there would be no violation of ERISA 406(a) or (b).

PTE 77-4 only addresses restrictions on sales commissions and investment management fees. The DOL released AO 93-12A and AO 93-13A, which address the bank's receipt of secondary servicing fees from a proprietary mutual fund. These AOs state that a proprietary mutual fund may pay the bank, or an affiliate of the bank, for secondary services provided to the mutual fund without a waiver or credit for a plan's pro rata share of such fees. Secondary services are defined as acting as a transfer agent or providing custodial, administrative, or accounting services. Neither PTE 77-4 nor the two AOs discuss the payment and receipt of 12b-1 fees. In AO 93-12A (footnote 4), however, the DOL indicates that at the time PTE 77-4 was granted, mutual funds were not permitted by the SEC to pay 12b-1 fees. Therefore, the DOL did not consider the payment and receipt of 12b-1 fees. The DOL stated, however, that it considers 12b-1 fees to be similar to sales commissions, which PTE 77-4 prohibits.

**12b-1 and other fees from nonproprietary funds—bank is directed trustee.** In AO 97-15A (Frost National Bank AO), the DOL concluded that the bank was a fiduciary when it advised plan sponsors regarding particular mutual funds in which to invest plan assets. In the view of the DOL, advising that plan assets be invested in mutual funds that pay 12b-1 or subtransfer agent fees to the bank violates ERISA 406(b)(1). The bank can avoid a violation of 406(b)(1) by

- disclosing to the plan the extent to which it may receive fees from the various mutual funds.
- having language in the trust agreement that any fees received by the bank as a result of the plan's investment in the various mutual funds will be used to pay all or a portion of the compensation that the plan is obligated to pay to the bank.
- offsetting on a dollar-per-dollar basis any fees the bank receives from the mutual funds against any fees that the plan owes to the bank.

There is also a potential 406(b)(3) violation the bank can mitigate by including in the trust agreement language that states the bank's receipt of fees from one or more mutual funds in connection with the plan's investment in such funds will be used to reduce the plan's obligation to the bank and will not increase the bank's compensation. This means that any fees that the bank received from the mutual funds that exceed the plan's liabilities must go to the plan.

**With respect to plans for which the bank does not provide any investment advice.** The plan sponsor and, in some instances, the plan participants select mutual funds in which to invest plan assets from among those made available by the bank. In these cases, the DOL states that the bank, as a directed trustee, is not exercising any authority or control to cause a plan to invest in a mutual fund so the receipt by the bank of a fee or other compensation from mutual funds in connection with such investment would not in and of itself violate ERISA

406(b)(3). Because the bank reserves the right to add or remove mutual fund families that it makes available to plans, however, the DOL could not conclude that the bank is not exercising any authority or control to cause a plan to invest in a mutual fund. The DOL found no violation of ERISA 406(b)(1) or (b)(3) in these situations as the bank's trustee agreements with the plans are structured so that any 12b-1 or subtransfer agent fees attributable to the plans' investments in mutual funds are used to benefit the plans, either as a dollar-for-dollar offset against the fees the plans would be obligated to pay to the bank for its services or as amounts credited directly to the plans.

In AO 97-15A, the DOL reminds plan sponsors that they have a responsibility under ERISA 404(a)(1) to act prudently and solely in the interest of plan participants and beneficiaries both in deciding whether to enter into, or continue, the trustee agreement with the bank and in determining which mutual funds to utilize or make available to plan participants and beneficiaries. Plan sponsors should determine that the compensation paid directly or indirectly by the plan to the bank is reasonable, taking into account the trustee services provided to the plan as well as any other fees or compensation received by the bank in connection with the investment of plan assets. Plan sponsors, to fulfill this responsibility, must obtain sufficient information regarding any fees or other compensation that the bank receives with respect to the plan's investments in each mutual fund to make an informed decision whether the bank's compensation for services is no more than reasonable. The plan sponsor should also periodically monitor the actions taken by the bank in the performance of its duties, to assure, among other things, that any fee offsets to which the plan is entitled are correctly calculated and applied.

**Note:** Under the ERISA 408(b)(2) regulations that were finalized in 2012, plan sponsors should receive the information (in the previous paragraph) that the DOL has deemed necessary in order for there to be no ERISA 406(b)(1) or (b)(3) violations.

**12b-1 and other fees from proprietary funds—bank is directed trustee.** In AO 2003-09A, the DOL concluded that a bank as directed trustee (in a bundled service arrangement) could accept 12b-1 and other fees from non-affiliated or proprietary funds (an affiliate of the bank is investment adviser to the funds) without violating ERISA 406(b)(1) or 406(b)(3) when the decision to invest in such funds is made by the plan sponsor or participant.

In the situation described in AO 2003-09A, the pricing arrangement between the bank and plan sponsors is for a bundled service that is predicated on a plan offering one or more proprietary funds as an investment option. Disclosures from the bank to the plan allow the plan sponsor to make an informed decision regarding the proprietary funds (and the fees paid to the bank from the funds). Plan sponsors then pick the funds in which their plan will invest. The bank does not restrict the mutual funds that a plan sponsor may utilize, beyond requiring, as a condition of engagement, that a plan select at least one proprietary fund to offer as an investment option. The bank will, if requested, provide a list of investment funds for the plan sponsor to consider. The plan sponsor is free to select funds other than those listed by the bank. The plan sponsor's choice of funds affects the cost of engaging the bank to provide plan services. For example, if the plan offers three proprietary funds, the cost of services that the bank will provide would cost less than if the plan offered two proprietary funds.

The bank asserted in AO 2003-09A that because the bank does not restrict the mutual funds that a plan may utilize, the preparation and furnishing of a list offering an array of mutual fund choices does not constitute discretion to add or delete mutual fund families in which plans may invest. The bank asserted that if a plan decides to remove a proprietary fund as an investment option, the bank's total revenue from the plan and proprietary fund would be affected, leaving less asset management revenue with which to provide plan services. If a plan did decide to remove a proprietary fund, the bank would invite the plan to consider one or more other proprietary funds to replace non-proprietary fund investment options. If the plan does not choose to offer another proprietary fund as an investment option, the bank would continue to provide plan services pursuant to the bundled services arrangement, but would reevaluate continuing the bundled arrangement under the current pricing structure. The bank would give the plan sponsor 60 days' written notice of a fee adjustment or 30 days' notice of termination of the arrangement.

The DOL concluded in AO 2003-09A that the bank's receipt of 12b-1 or subtransfer agent fees from mutual funds, including proprietary funds, under the circumstances described by the bank would not violate ERISA 406(b)(1) or (b)(3) when the decision to invest in such funds is made by the plan sponsor or by plan participants.

**12b-1 and other fees from nonproprietary funds—recordkeeper.** In AO 97-16A (Aetna AO), the DOL stated that a determination of whether a person or entity is a fiduciary with respect to a plan requires an analysis of the types of functions performed and actions taken by the person or entity on behalf of the plan to determine whether particular functions or actions are fiduciary in nature and therefore subject to ERISA's fiduciary responsibility provisions. In AO 97-16A, the DOL acknowledged that Aetna was not a fiduciary because Aetna was providing recordkeeping and other administrative services. The DOL also stated that a person would not be exercising discretionary authority or control over the management of a plan or its assets (and thus becoming a fiduciary) solely as a result of deleting or substituting a fund from a program of investment options and services offered to plans, provided that the appropriate plan fiduciary in fact makes the decision to accept or reject the change. In this regard, the fiduciary must be provided advance notice of the change, including any changes in the fees received, and afforded a reasonable period of time within which to decide whether to accept or reject the change and, in the event of a rejection, secure a new service provider. Aetna stated that it provides the plan sponsor advance notice of the deletion or substitution of funds and a reasonable period of time following receipt of the notice (120 days) within which to reject the change in funds and secure a new service provider. The DOL concluded in AO 97-16A that Aetna would not become a fiduciary under these circumstances so the acceptance of 12b-1 and other fees from the mutual funds would not cause any prohibited transaction violations.

**Are revenue-sharing payments plan assets?** The DOL issued AO 2013-03A to address the question of whether revenue-sharing payments are considered plan assets under ERISA. The question was submitted by Principal Life Insurance Company, which acts as a recordkeeper for participant-directed DC plans and receives 12b-1, shareholder, and other administrative service fees from affiliated and unaffiliated mutual funds. Although Principal retains all of the fees, it may agree with a client plan to maintain a bookkeeping record of revenue sharing received in connection with the plan's investments. Sometimes this arrangement is referred to as an "ERISA budget." The bookkeeping account reflects credits to the plan calculated by reference to the estimated revenue-sharing payments. Principal then applies the credits to pay certain plan expenses, such as for the services of accountants, consultants, actuaries, or attorneys to the plan. Alternatively, Principal may agree to deposit an amount equal to the credits directly into a plan account, periodically or on specified dates.

Principal deposits the revenue-sharing payments into its general asset accounts and does not establish a special bank or custodial account to hold the revenue-sharing payments. Principal makes no representations that revenue-sharing amounts it receives will be set aside for the benefit of the plan or represent a separate fund for payment of benefits or expense under the plan.

The DOL was asked whether the revenue-sharing payments are considered plan assets under ERISA. The DOL responded in AO 2013-03A that the amounts recorded in the bookkeeping account as representing revenue-sharing payments are not plan assets. The plan's contractual right to receive the amounts as agreed to with Principal or to have the payments applied to plan expenses would be an asset of the plan. If the assets were held in trust on behalf of the plan, in a separate account with a bank in the name of the plan, or plan documents specified that separately maintained funds belong to the plan, then the assets would be an asset of the plan as the actions and representations of the parties involved would lead to this conclusion.

The AO cautioned plan sponsors, however, stating that they must act prudently and in the best interests of plan participants and beneficiaries in the negotiation of the specific formula and methodology under which revenue sharing will be credited to the plan and paid back to the plan or to plan service providers. Plan sponsors should understand the formula, methodology, and assumptions used in arriving at the amounts to be returned to the plan or used to pay plan service providers following disclosure of all relevant information pertaining to the proposed arrangement. Plan sponsors must be capable of periodically monitoring the actions taken in the performance of its duties to assure, among other things, that any amounts to which the plan may be entitled under the terms of the arrangement are correctly calculated and applied for the benefit of the plan. Plan sponsors should take into account its ability to oversee the service provider, including its ability to oversee and monitor the service provider's determinations under the formula. In addition, plan sponsors must obtain sufficient information to ensure that any service providers to the plan who are paid directly are paid no more than reasonable compensation for the services provided by them to the plan.

## Float

Many banks retain "float" as part of their compensation. Float is the cash value earned from accounts established on the retail side of the bank for the short-term investment of plan assets pending investment direction or until distribution or disbursement checks are presented for payment. The DOL issued FAB 2002-3, November 5, 2002, regarding the retention of float as part of the bank's compensation. FAB 2002-3 also lists all the obligations of the plan sponsor and of the bank as directed trustee to retain float without violating ERISA 406(b)(1).

It is important to note that in addition to following all the conditions in FAB 2002-3, banks retaining float must provide adequate disclosure under the service provider disclosure regulation at 408(b)(2) as well as Schedule C of Form 5500.

FAB 2002-3 quoted from AO 93-24A and an informational letter dated August 11, 1994, to the American Bankers Association in which the DOL stated that if a directed trustee has openly negotiated with the plan fiduciary to retain float attributable to outstanding benefit checks as part of its overall compensation, then the bank's use of the float would not be considered self-dealing. This conclusion was reached because the bank would not be exercising its fiduciary authority or control for its own benefit. To avoid problems, banks should, as part of their fee negotiations, provide full and fair disclosure regarding the use of float. The primary issue for banks with float arrangements is whether the bank has disclosed to its plan sponsor customers sufficient information concerning the administration of its accounts holding float so that the customer can reasonably approve the arrangement based on an understanding of the bank's compensation. The arrangement also must not permit the bank to affect the amount of its compensation by giving the bank broad discretion over the duration of the float.

The DOL is very specific as to what must be included in the service agreement between the bank and the plan sponsor in regards to float. The bank expecting to retain float as part of its compensation must

- disclose to the plan fiduciary the specific circumstances for how the bank earns and retains float.
- in the case of float on contributions pending investment direction, establish, disclose, and adhere to specific time frames within which cash pending investment direction will be invested following direction from the plan fiduciary, as well as any exceptions that might apply.
- in the case of float on distributions, disclose when the float period commences (e.g., when the check is requested, written, and mailed) and ends (when the check is presented for payment). Also, disclose and adhere to the time frames for mailing and any other administrative practices that might affect the duration of the float period.
- disclose to the plan fiduciary the rate of the float or the specific manner used to determine that rate. For example, earnings on cash pending investment and earnings on uncashed checks are generally at a money market interest rate.
- provide to the plan fiduciary periodic statements or reports of distribution checks to determine the extent to which checks tend to remain outstanding for unusually long periods of time (e.g., 90 days or more).

## Soft Dollars

The concept of using client commissions to pay broker-dealers for research services is often referred to as "soft dollars." As fiduciaries, money managers are obligated to act in the best interest of their clients and cannot use client commissions to benefit themselves, absent client consent. Money managers who obtain research services from broker-dealers with soft dollars are not paying for those services with their own funds, which benefits the money manager and creates a conflict of interest in selecting which broker-dealer to execute the client's trades. Section 28(e) of the Securities Exchange Act of 1934 establishes a safe harbor for money managers who use client commissions to purchase research services for their managed accounts. Under section 28(e), a money manager is protected from liability for a breach of fiduciary duty solely on the basis of having paid more than the lowest commission rate for "both brokerage and research services provided by a broker-dealer," if the money manager determines in good faith that the amount of the commission is reasonable in relation to the value of the services provided by the broker-dealer.

The SEC has issued guidance regarding the analysis of whether the brokerage and research services fall within the safe harbor. The analysis requires these three-steps:

- Do the brokerage and research services offered by the broker-dealer constitute eligible brokerage and research under section 28(e)?
- Do the brokerage and research services offered by the broker-dealer provide appropriate assistance in the performance of the money manager's decision-making responsibilities?
- Can the money manager make a good-faith determination that the amount of commission paid is reasonable in light of the value of the brokerage and research services that are obtained from the broker-dealer?

Banks that are fiduciaries to retirement plans that engage in soft-dollar arrangements may be engaging in a prohibited transaction.

The DOL has issued ERISA Technical Release No. 86-1, which describes various soft-dollar scenarios that do not result in prohibited transaction violations under ERISA.

The DOL notes that section 28(e) of the Securities Exchange Act of 1934 permits the soft-dollar practice and authorizes a "safe harbor" if a person who exercises investment discretion with respect to a securities transaction receives bona fide research services and if the commission is reasonable in relation to the value of the research services provided by the broker-dealer. The safe harbor of section 28(e) does not cover directed brokerage arrangements. A directed brokerage arrangement is one in which the plan fiduciary directs an investment manager to use a particular broker-dealer and the broker-dealer agrees to pay the expenses of the plan or give the plan brokerage and research services. The SEC updated section 28(e) in 2006, as noted in OCC Bulletin 2007-7, "Soft Dollar Guidance: Use of Commission Payments by Fiduciaries."

ERISA Technical Release No. 86-1 goes on to describe various directed brokerage arrangements that do not result in a prohibited transaction violation, although they may fall outside of the safe harbor of section 28(e). When a plan fiduciary instructs an investment manager to enter a directed brokerage arrangement with a specific broker-dealer, the fiduciary is responsible for ensuring that the value of the brokerage and research services received by the plan is at least equal in value to the commissions paid by the plan. In addition, the fiduciary has the responsibility to monitor the execution of trades and determine that the commissions paid are reasonable in relation to the brokerage and research services provided to the plan. If the directed brokerage arrangement involves more than one plan, the fiduciary is responsible for each plan.

Banks should have appropriate controls in place to make sure that when they engage in soft-dollar arrangements they do not violate ERISA or 12 CFR 9 for national banks and 12 CFR 150 for federal savings associations. In addition, banks must include soft dollars as compensation that is disclosed under the service provider disclosure regulation at 408(b)(2) as well as Schedule C of Form 5500.

## Overdrafts

An essential part of the bank's custodial or trustee services (or as investment manager for plans or as investment manager to collective funds in which retirement plans invest) is the orderly processing of the plan's securities and other financial market transactions. Such processing revolves around the anticipated receipt of funds to cover the purchase of securities.

On occasion, an account may not receive funds as intended because of errors, unexpected delays by a counterparty or its agent, settlement failures by a counterparty or its custodian, broker-dealer failures, or inefficient markets. When these situations arise, banks generally settle transactions without contemporaneous assurance that the plan has enough funds, in the correct currency. This "overdraft protection" is an extension of credit between the bank and the retirement plan. Unlike a conventional loan between a plan and the bank, overdraft protection involves no agreement to lend a stated sum for a specific period of time. Events giving rise to an overdraft are generally inadvertent or outside the control of the bank or affiliate. The provision of overdraft protection may result in a prohibited transaction under ERISA 406(a) and (b).

The DOL, in AO 2003-02A, indicated that in its view the provision of overdraft protection services appears to be necessary to ensure the orderly processing of plan securities transactions and other financial markets transactions, as well as a banking practice recognized and permitted by federal banking authorities. As such, overdraft protection services constitute an "ancillary service" under ERISA 408(b)(6) and would not constitute a prohibited transaction violation under ERISA 406.

The bank must comply with the statutory exemptions of ERISA 408(b)(2) or 408(b)(6) when providing overdraft protection services, and the provision of the overdraft services must not be part of an arrangement to secure credit unrelated to the settlement of securities. If providing overdraft services results in additional revenue to a bank, the bank must include the revenue as compensation that is disclosed under the service provider disclosure regulation at 408(b)(2) as well as Schedule C of Form 5500.

Banks that extend overdraft protection services to retirement plans must establish controls that ensure

- plan fiduciaries are fully informed about and approve the terms governing the provision of overdraft protection services.
- fee disclosure documents are clear that charges attendant to overdrafts are in addition to, and separate from, fees charged for other services, such as trustee or investment management services, provided by the bank or an affiliate.
- banks establish and follow policies and procedures relating to overdraft protection services, including measures designed to ensure timely notice to the appropriate plan fiduciary of any overdraft and the imposition of any overdraft charges.
- banks establish and follow policies and procedures that require monitoring of overdraft charges and that limit the duration and usage of overdraft services.
- banks establish and follow policies and procedures that limit the ability of an investment manager or other fiduciary to utilize overdraft protection services as a routine means by which securities transactions are settled.

If a bank is concerned with prohibited transactions related to an extension of credit to an IRA, then the bank may want to look at the provisions of PTE 80-26. PTE 80-26 provides relief from IRC section 4975(c)(1)(B) with respect to an "extension of credit." PTE 80-26 permits parties in interest with respect to employee benefit plans (which includes an IRA) to make certain loans and extensions of credit to such plans. As stated in AO 2011-09A, relief is available under the class exemption for extensions of credit described in IRC 4975(c)(1)(B) to the extent the conditions of the class exemption are met.

## Sweep Fees

Banks typically offer "sweep services" to invest excess cash in employee benefit plans for which banks act as custodians or directed trustees. A sweep service may occur on a daily, weekly, or other basis. Depending on how the arrangement is structured, charging an additional fee for the provision of a sweep service may involve one or more prohibited transaction violations under ERISA 406(a) and (b). There may, however, be statutory relief for these prohibited transaction violations under ERISA 408(b)(2) or 408(b)(6).

The DOL has indicated in two AO letters, 2003-02A and 2001-10A, that the provision of sweep services by a trustee who is subject to direction from an independent investment manager for the investment of plan assets may constitute an "ancillary service" within the meaning of the statutory exemption found at ERISA 408(b)(6). The AOs point out that a service is ancillary if it aids or is auxiliary to a primary or principal service. The AOs also state that what constitutes an ancillary service within the meaning of ERISA 408(b)(6) depends on the expectations of the parties, as evidenced by the terms of the underlying service agreement and applicable federal banking law. The ancillary services exemption at ERISA 408(b)(6) provides relief for violations of ERISA 406(b).

Sweep services seem to fall under the statutory exemption found at ERISA 408(b)(2), according to AO 88-02A, and a DOL information letter issued to Robert S. Plotkin, dated

August 1, 1986. ERISA 408(b)(2) exempts from the prohibitions of section 406(a) contracting (or making reasonable arrangements) for services (or a combination of services) with a party in interest if (1) the service is necessary for the establishment or operation of the plan; (2) the service is furnished under a contract that is reasonable; and (3) no more than reasonable compensation is paid for the service. DOL regulations clarify the terms "necessary service" (29 CFR 2550.408b-2(b)), "reasonable contract or arrangement" (29 CFR 2550.408b-2(c)), and "reasonable compensation" (29 CFR 2550.408c-2). A bank must include any revenue it receives from sweep services as compensation that is disclosed under the service provider disclosure regulation at 408(b)(2) as well as Schedule C of Form 5500.

The Plotkin letter describes the following arrangements for sweep services, which illustrate the application of the 408(b)(2) exemption to a sweep arrangement in a manner that the DOL concluded would qualify for relief under the exemption:

- The bank provides sweep services to plans under a single-fee arrangement, calculated as a percentage of the market value of the plan funds under management. There are no separate charges for the provision of sweep services.
- The bank includes a provision in the trust agreement with the plan customer that the bank will provide sweep services so that, at the close of each business day, the bank is required to sweep all uninvested cash in excess of $100 into the bank's money market fund. For this service, the bank charges the plan a fee calculated as a percentage of the daily invested cash balance in the money market fund. The bank has no investment discretion in regard to fund withdrawals. The plan's arrangement with the bank is subject to immediate termination without penalty and requires the bank to notify the plan no less than 30 days before any change in sweep service fees.

## Gains From the Correction of Trading Errors

Banks acting as a recordkeeper or trustee to employee benefit plans typically experience occasional errors in processing investment transactions on behalf of client plans. These errors may occur when purchase or sale orders are placed for an erroneous amount of investment or when such orders are not completed at the correct time. Banks typically undertake to make the employee benefit plan whole by placing corrective purchase or sale orders. The price of the investments will likely have changed during the interim between the erroneous trade and the corrective trade. As a result, a gain or a loss may be generated due to the correction.

Banks should have policies and procedures in place that state that the bank will fund any losses to the plan or plan participant resulting from the correction of trading errors.

The DOL announced on February 4, 2013, that it had reached a settlement agreement with ING Life Insurance and Annuity Co. regarding ING's practice of keeping investment gains resulting from the correction of trading errors. ING had a policy to correct inadvertent errors resulting from the incorrect or untimely processing of transactions for its ERISA plan clients or plan participants by absorbing losses and keeping gains. The DOL, after an investigation, determined that ING did not disclose its policy to its employee benefit plan customers. The

DOL then alleged that ING's failure to disclose its policy of keeping gains resulting from correcting trading errors was a failure to disclose compensation. As part of the settlement with ING, ING must make full disclosure of its investment transaction policy. The policy goes into some detail as to how ING corrects trading errors and how gains or losses may be generated from the correction of the trading error. The policy must be in writing. Disclosure of the policy must be made either through a separate notice for current clients or by incorporation into a future service contract for prospective clients. Current plan clients are given the opportunity to object to the policy within 30 days of notice. ING is also obligated to inform clients that it will track, on an annual basis, the effect that trade error corrections have on each plan and will make this information available to the client upon request. ING must also acknowledge that any gains that are kept under the correction policy constitute additional compensation for services that ING provides. ING must then report this additional compensation in accordance with the ERISA 408(b)(2) regulations.

The DOL has asserted that it is using its policy on the treatment of float as a basis for its treatment of gains resulting from the correction of trading errors. As a result, banks should provide full and fair disclosure (similar to the disclosure required under FAB 2002-3) to plan fiduciaries of the bank's receipt of compensation if the bank chooses to keep any gains resulting from the correction of trading errors. Full and fair disclosure must go into some detail as to how the bank will correct trading errors and how gains or losses may be generated from the correction of the trading error. The bank must also track, on an annual basis, corrections of trading errors for each plan and make this information available to the plan fiduciary and examiners upon request.

# Operational Control Processes

Basic control processes for the operational activities banks perform as part of the products and services they offer to retirement plans should be an integral part of each product and service. Control processes for retirement plan products and services should cover opening and maintaining individual participant accounts, receiving employer contributions and recording them to individual participant accounts, payment of plan expenses, plan asset valuations, buying and selling plan assets, providing Schedule C (for Form 5500) and 408(b)(2) information to plan fiduciaries, processing benefit distributions, and crediting and processing plan loans, as applicable. These are all operational activities that banks as trustee or recordkeeper may perform for retirement plans. Banks should document all the operational activities that they have agreed to provide to a retirement plan in a contract or other form of service-level agreement.

## Employer Contributions

The plan should receive employer contributions in a timely manner. If the plan does not receive these funds when plan documents indicate they are due and owing to the plan, the funds are delinquent and the employer is at fault.

Funds withheld from participant wages or paid to the employer are plan assets as of the earliest date on which the contributions can reasonably be segregated from the employer's general assets. Under ERISA regulations, 29 CFR 2510.3-102, an employer will have engaged in a prohibited transaction in violation of ERISA 406 if it continues to hold participant contributions commingled with the employer's general assets after the participant contributions reasonably could have been segregated. The "reasonably could have been segregated" date can be no later than the 15th business day of the month following the month in which participant contribution amounts are withheld from the employee's paychecks or paid to the employer. This is a maximum time period, not a safe harbor. There is a safe harbor available for plans with less than 100 participants. In these plans, participant contributions that are deposited no later than the seventh business day following the date they would have been paid in cash to participants are deemed to have been contributed to the plan on the earliest date they could be segregated from general assets. The effect of participant contributions becoming plan assets is twofold. First, ERISA requires that all plan assets be held in trust. If the employer does not timely forward participant contributions to the trust then it is in violation of ERISA's trust requirement. Second, an employer that fails to timely deposit participant contributions has engaged in a prohibited transaction.

The responsibilities of named fiduciaries and trustees of employee benefit plans for the collection of delinquent employer and employee contributions were laid out by the DOL in FAB 2008-01. The question the FAB addressed was whether, and to what extent, trust agreements and other instruments could exclude banks (and other fiduciaries) from responsibility for monitoring the plans' receipt of contributions, determining when they are delinquent, and taking appropriate steps for collection.

Under the FAB, if the trust instrument does not designate who is responsible for monitoring and collecting contributions under the terms of the trust instrument, then the directed trustee would have an obligation under ERISA 404 and 405(a) to take appropriate steps to remedy a situation where the trustee knows that no party has assumed responsibility for the collection and monitoring of contributions and that delinquent contributions are going uncollected.

The FAB goes on to state that a directed trustee as fiduciary should take "reasonable efforts" under the circumstances to remedy this situation to shield itself from co-fiduciary liability under ERISA 405(a)(3) if the bank has knowledge of a breach of another fiduciary. Reasonable efforts to remedy the situation include advising the named fiduciary or the DOL of the breach, reporting the breach to other fiduciaries of the plan, seeking an amendment of the relevant plan and trust documents, or seeking a court order mandating a proper allocation of fiduciary responsibilities over contributions. Banks should adopt policies and procedures that first notify the employer of a delinquent contribution situation, monitoring the employer's response, and then, if not satisfied, consulting with internal or external counsel to determine if notification of delinquent contributions should be given to the DOL. Notification of delinquent contribution situations may be given to the DOL by sending a letter or e-mail to the director of the appropriate DOL regional office (as found on the DOL's Web site, www.dol.gov/ebsa) and providing the director with information on the plan's history of delinquent contributions.

Bank trustees should also ensure that their trust agreements appropriately allocate the responsibility for monitoring and collecting delinquent contributions.

## Paying Plan Expenses

The operation of an employee benefit plan involves various fees and expenses. There may be fees for trustees, investment managers or advisers, lawyers, accountants, auditors, and actuaries.

A determination as to whether to pay a particular expense out of plan assets is a fiduciary act governed by ERISA's fiduciary responsibility provisions. The DOL has a long-standing position (AO 2001-01A) that there is a class of activities that relate to the formation of plans, and these are referred to as settlor expenses. Settlor expenses cannot be paid from plan assets. These would include expenses related to the establishment, design, and termination of the plan.

Fiduciary expenses are the ongoing expenses associated with administering the plan. The plan sponsor may pay fiduciary expenses directly, or the plan may pay the expenses under certain conditions. Examples of expenses that are fiduciary in nature and generally eligible for payment from plan assets include the following:

- Recordkeeping.
- Legal, auditing, and annual reporting.
- Mandatory participant disclosures.
- Extra participant communications that are helpful but not legally required.
- Benefit estimates, benefit calculations, and actuarial calculations.
- Compliance costs for maintaining the tax-qualified status of a plan, e.g., amendments to comply with new regulations.
- TPA expenses.
- Pension Benefit Guaranty Corporation (PBGC) premiums.

In addition to determining whether expenses of the plan are settlor expenses or fiduciary expenses, a determination must also be made as to whether all the services being provided to the plan are "reasonable." Any ongoing arrangement for services to a plan must satisfy the requirements under the "reasonable services" exemption to the prohibited transaction rules. This is because any provider of services to the plan is a party in interest as soon as it begins providing services. The service arrangement must meet the reasonable services exemption or there will be a prohibited transaction. The requirements for the reasonable and necessary services exemption in ERISA 408(b)(2) are that

- the service must be necessary for the operation of the plan. (A service is necessary for the plan's operation if it is appropriate and helpful in carrying out the purposes for which the plan is established or maintained.)
- the service must be furnished under a contract or an arrangement that is reasonable.
- the plan may pay no more than reasonable compensation for the service.

The plan fiduciary must determine whether these requirements are met both initially and upon renewal of the service provider's contract.

The decision of the plan fiduciary to pay expenses from plan assets is a fiduciary decision subject to the fiduciary duty rules of ERISA. Before using plan assets to pay the costs of services provided to the plan, the plan sponsor or other designated fiduciary should determine the following:

- The plan document permits the payment of the expense. Plan documents for individual account plans, such as 401(k) plans, may set out the method for allocating expenses paid by the plan to participant accounts.
- The goods, services, and associated expenses relate to fiduciary and not to settlor decisions. Plan sponsors act as a settlor in establishing and designing a retirement plan but also act as a fiduciary when administering the plan. When an employer chooses the terms of its retirement plan, it is acting as a settlor, but when it administers the plan, it is acting as a fiduciary. The employer, and not the plan, must pay for settlor expenses. Expenses for trustee, recordkeeper, and investment manager services are all expenses the plan may pay if permitted by the plan document.
- The expenditure is prudent and the amount is reasonable. Plan fiduciaries should understand all of the direct and indirect compensation service providers would receive in connection with the plan services. They should also thoroughly understand the provided services. Finally, when selecting a service provider, the plan fiduciary should also understand how the proposed fees and services compare with other providers available in the marketplace.

When an employer maintains more than one plan and hires a service provider to provide services to all of the employer's plans, each plan must pay only those expenses that it properly incurs and may not pay expenses properly allocable to another plan, even if maintained by the same employer.

The method for allocating expenses among participants in a defined contribution plan may be set out in the plan document. Where the method of allocation is set forth in the plan document, fiduciaries are required to follow the prescribed allocation method.

When the plan documents are silent or ambiguous on this issue, fiduciaries must select the method for allocating plan expenses. According to FAB 2003-3, "Allocation of Expenses in a Defined Contribution Plan," plan sponsors and fiduciaries have considerable discretion to determine how to allocate plan expenses among participant accounts. A plan fiduciary must be prudent in the selection of the method of allocation. Prudence requires a process by which the fiduciary weighs the competing interests of various classes of plan participants and the effects of the various allocation methods on those interests. A method of allocation can favor one class of participants over another, if the fiduciary has a rational basis for selecting the allocation method. In addition, the allocation of different types of expenses can use different methods.

Plan fiduciaries use two common methods of allocation:

- **Pro rata:** The pro rata method allocates a portion of plan expenses to each individual account, based on the amount of assets in each account. This method may be reasonable when fees or charges to the plan are determined on the basis of account balances (for example, investment management fees).

- **Per capita:** This method charges expenses equally to each account without regard to the assets in each individual account. This may be a reasonable method of allocating certain fixed administrative expenses of the plan (such as recordkeeping, legal, auditing, annual reporting, and claims processing expenses). When fees or charges to the plan are determined on the basis of account balances, such as investment management fees, a per capita method of allocating such expenses among all participants would appear arbitrary.

With regard to services that provide investment advice to individual participants, a fiduciary may be able to justify the allocation of such expenses on either a pro rata or a per capita basis and without regard to actual utilization of the services by particular individual accounts. Investment advice services might also be charged on a utilization basis, whereby the expense will be allocated to an individual account solely on the basis of a participant's utilization of the service.

There are certain expenses which may be charged solely to a particular participant's individual account, rather than allocated among the accounts of all participants (e.g., on a pro rata or per capita basis). Under 29 CFR 2520.102-3(l), plans are required to include in the summary plan description a summary of any provisions that may result in the imposition of a fee or charge on a participant or beneficiary, or the individual account thereof, the payment of which is a condition to the receipt of benefits under the plan. Examples of these specific plan expenses are

- hardship withdrawals.
- calculation of benefits payable under different plan distribution options.
- benefit distributions.
- accounts of separated vested participants.
- qualified domestic relations orders and qualified medical child support order determinations.

Questions as to how to pay plan expenses using revenue-sharing payments has been addressed by the DOL in AO 2013-03A. A complete discussion on "ERISA Budgets" and revenue-sharing payments can be found in the "Compensation Issues" section of this booklet, under the subsection "Are revenue-sharing payments plan assets?"

Banks should be aware of AO 79-49, which permits a bank to serve as the trustee of the bank's pension plan without prohibited transaction consequences. AO 79-49 references 29 CFR 2550.408b-2, which exempts from the prohibitions of ERISA 406(a) payment by a plan to a party in interest, including a fiduciary (e.g., a bank acting as trustee for the bank's own pension plans), for any service provided the service is necessary for the establishment or operations of the plan; the service is furnished under a contract or arrangement that is reasonable; and no more than reasonable compensation is paid for the service. In order to also avoid the prohibitions of ERISA 406(b), under 29 CFR 2550.408b-2(e)(3), a bank acting as trustee for its own pension plan must provide the trustee services without the receipt of compensation or other consideration (other than reimbursement of direct expenses properly and actually incurred in the performance of the trustee services). There are many helpful examples at 29 CFR 2550.408b-2(f) that demonstrate these concepts.

In AO 97-19A, the DOL answered the question of whether a company (which could be a bank) providing services to its own pension plan may receive fees from certain mutual funds that the company has selected as investment options for participants as reimbursement for direct expenses incurred in providing services to its own plan. The investment options that are available to plan participants include non-affiliated mutual funds and proprietary mutual funds. The fees received from the mutual funds are either 12b-1 fees or subtransfer agent fees. The company wants to begin accepting the fees payable to it by the non-affiliated mutual funds in connection with plan investments as reimbursement of the expenses it incurs in providing recordkeeping and other administrative services to the plan (another entity serves as trustee), which amounts would otherwise be paid to the company directly from the plan's assets in accordance with the terms of the plan.

The company represented to the DOL that it has developed methods for determining the dollar amount of its reasonable direct expenses incurred in the provision of services to the plan within the meaning of 29 CFR 2550.408c-2(b)(3). The company will only seek reimbursement for expenses that the company would not incur but for its provision of services to the plan, e.g., salary and benefits paid to certain employees who are engaged full time to provide administrative services to the plan and whose position would be terminated if the company should cease providing services to the plan; charges for telephone services dedicated to answering participant inquiries and taking participant investment directions; and the cost of office supplies, including paper stocks for printing participant information materials, used in connection with the provision of services to the plan. The company anticipated that the aggregate of fees that it will receive from the non-affiliated mutual funds will not exceed its reasonable direct expenses. Any fees earned in excess of what is required to reimburse the company for its direct expenses will be applied to the provision of additional services to the plan, passed through to the plan, or waived by the company.

The DOL, in AO 97-19A, stated that if the company credits all payments received from the non-affiliated mutual funds in connection with investments directed by plan participants exactly against its "direct expenses" incurred in providing services to the plan, for which the plan would otherwise be liable, and provided that the company receives no compensation or other consideration for such services, the company would not violate ERISA 406(b)(3).

## Proxy Voting

The DOL, in an interpretive bulletin relating to the exercise of shareholder rights and written statements of investment policy, including proxy voting policies or guidelines (IB 29 CFR 2509.08-2), has taken the position that proxy voting is integral to the fiduciary act of managing plan assets. The bulletin states that the responsibility for voting proxies lies exclusively with the plan trustee, except when the trustee is subject to the direction of a named fiduciary, or when an investment manager has the power to manage plan assets. In voting proxies, whoever has the obligation to vote the proxy must consider only those factors that relate to the economic value of the plan's investment.

If the responsible fiduciary reasonably determines that the cost of voting (including the cost of research, if necessary, to determine how to vote) is likely to exceed the expected economic benefits of voting, or if the exercise of voting results in the imposition of unwarranted trading or other restrictions, the fiduciary has an obligation to refrain from voting.

The investment manager, or other responsible fiduciary that is voting the proxies, is required to maintain accurate records as to their proxy voting decisions, including, where appropriate, a cost-benefit analysis.

The statement of investment policy, maintained on behalf of the plan, may contain guidelines or general instructions regarding proxy voting decisions.

ESOPs have certain requirements regarding proxy voting that are contained in IRC 409(e). ESOPs, unlike other defined contribution plans, must pass through voting rights on allocated shares to the participants. If the company is publicly traded, each participant or beneficiary is entitled to direct the plan on how to vote the shares (on all issues) allocated to the participant or beneficiary. If the company is not publicly traded, each participant or beneficiary is entitled to direct the plan on how to vote the shares (on only major issues such as mergers, consolidation, and recapitalization) allocated to that participant or beneficiary.

Many trust documents contain pass-through voting provisions under which a trustee must follow the timely voting instructions of plan participants with respect to the shares of company stock allocated to participants' accounts. When the trustee does not receive timely instructions from the plan participants, it may vote allocated but non-directed shares in accordance with Revenue Ruling 95-57.

On some proxy issues, in order to avoid a charge of favoring the plan sponsor over the interests of the participants and beneficiaries, particularly when dealing with plans covering the bank's employees, the bank may elect to hire an independent fiduciary to vote shares to eliminate any perceived conflict.

## Processing Benefit Payments and Withholding Taxes

Processing benefit payments, withholding taxes, and preparing IRS Form 1099-R are administrative services that banks provide. When the bank provides participant recordkeeping services, it calculates the distribution amount and processes the benefit payments. Types of payments to participants and beneficiaries include the following:

- Lump sum or periodic payments (minimum required distribution payments must generally begin by age 70½).
- Hardship or other in-service withdrawal (if specified in the defined contribution plan document).
- Distributions subject to a qualified domestic relations order (QDRO).
- Distributions of accrued benefits at termination of employment.
- Early withdrawals (before age 59½) that may be subject to a 10 percent penalty.

Banks should establish policies and procedures for processing distributions that include all the above payment types, plus any others provided for in the plan documents. Banks should have controls that ensure proper approval and conformance to the plan document for each payment. If the bank serves as recordkeeper, service agreements may require the bank to engage in an individual evaluation of each hardship withdrawal or QDRO distribution. This evaluation may involve the interpretation of legal documents. When required, banks should monitor the age of plan participants as well as IRA owners in order to ensure compliance with minimum distribution requirements.

Banks should also have policies and procedures that address the taxation of retirement plan distributions. Generally, the IRC treats all qualified plan and traditional IRA distributions as ordinary taxable income upon receipt. Favorable tax consequences are available, however, for certain types of plan distributions.

A participant who receives an "eligible rollover distribution" may defer the taxation of the distribution by transferring all or any portion of the distribution to another qualified plan or IRA within 60 days after receiving the distribution. Such a transfer is a rollover. The portion rolled over is generally not subject to income taxation until the plan or IRA subsequently distributes any of these assets to the participant. Some distributions are not eligible for rollover. There are many rules in IRC 402(c) that apply in order for the participant to receive this deferral of taxation. Rollovers are reported to the IRS and the participant on Form 1099-R.

The IRC requires withholding for federal income taxes at a 20 percent flat rate for any eligible rollover distribution over $200 that is not rolled over. In order to ensure participants have information about making direct rollovers (and thereby avoiding the 20 percent mandatory withholding), the plan fiduciary must provide an explanation notice to the recipient of an eligible rollover distribution no more than 180 days and no fewer than 30 days before making the distribution. The notice explains the rollover rules, the special tax treatment for lump sum distributions, the direct rollover option, and the mandatory 20 percent withholding rules. The notice also explains how distributions from the IRA that is receiving the rollover may have different restrictions and tax consequences than the retirement plan distribution. The IRS has provided safe harbor models for the explanation notice (IRS Notice 2009-68).

## Processing Participant Loans

Participant loans are an optional feature for defined contribution plans, most often 401(k) plans. Defined benefit plans may not have participant loans, and IRA owners may not borrow from IRA assets. Bank trustees distribute loan proceeds from plan assets, as directed by the plan fiduciary and deposit loan repayments. When the bank is also the participant recordkeeper, additional duties customarily include calculating the maximum loan amount and preparing loan documents.

Paperless loans are very common, although they may not be used for plans where a joint and survivor annuity is the default form of distribution and spousal consent is required for any distribution. With a paperless loan, execution of the loan disbursement check constitutes signing of the loan promissory note. Automated participant loan processes through a voice response unit or a Web site are common.

Plan documents must authorize participant loans and they must be consistent with a participant loan policy. While there is no requirement that each plan must offer participant loans, ERISA includes a statutory exemption from the prohibited transaction rules that enables plans to offer loans to participant employees. The statutory exemption, 29 CFR 2550.408b-1, contains numerous restrictions that limit the loan amount, loan terms, interest rate, and availability of plan loans. Plan loans must also meet the restrictions at IRC 72(p) in order for the loan amount not to be deemed a distribution subject to income tax. Plan loans may not exceed $50,000; the loans must be repayable within five years, with the exception of loans used to acquire a principal residence of the participant; and payments are to be made no less frequently than quarterly.

The plan fiduciary considers all of these restrictions in the creation of the participant loan policy. A typical participant loan policy contains the following information:

- Identity of the party responsible for administering the loan policy (usually the plan administrator).
- Procedure for applying for a loan.
- Basis on which loans are approved or denied.
- Limitations (if any) on the types and amount of loans offered.
- Procedure for determining a reasonable interest rate.
- Definition of eligible collateral.
- Events constituting default and the steps that will be taken in the event of default.

Plan fiduciaries should have controls in place to ensure that participant loans comply with the plan, loan policy, and legal requirements. Banks that act as recordkeepers should obtain proper approval of loans before issuance, including spousal consent (for plans subject to survivor annuity requirements).

The Federal Reserve Board, in a change to Regulation Z that was effective July 1, 2010, has provided an exemption from the truth in lending disclosures for loans from retirement plans. Under 12 CFR 226.3(g), an extension of credit to a participant in an IRC 401(a) tax qualified plan, 403(b) plan, or 457(b) plan will be exempt from Regulation Z if the loan is comprised of fully vested funds from the participant's account and complies with IRC 72 and other requirements under the IRC.

Another law applies when a plan participant is in the military and has a loan. The Servicemembers Civil Relief Act (SCRA) applies to pension plan loans. Under the SCRA, creditors, including a pension plan, are required to drop interest rates down to no more than 6 percent on debt owed by those entering military service for the period of such military service. The loan will not fail to be a qualified loan under ERISA solely because the interest rate is capped by SCRA. Under SCRA, a plan fiduciary could petition a court to retain a higher rate based on the individual's ability to pay. Under the Uniformed Services

Employment and Reemployment Rights Act, a plan may, but is not required to, suspend the obligation to make regular loan repayments to the plan during the period of active military service.

If the bank acts as recordkeeper for the plan, it may agree to monitor repayment of loans and send a report of delinquent loans to the employer. When a participant fails to make the required payments when due, a "deemed distribution" of the remaining balance of the loan occurs at the time of the default. The plan may allow the participant a "cure period" in which to make a required installment payment (and avoid a deemed distribution). The close of the cure period triggers a deemed distribution. The cure period may not extend beyond the last day of the calendar quarter following the calendar quarter in which the required installment payment was due (26 CFR 1.72(p)-1, Q&A-10). A plan fiduciary typically informs the bank acting as a directed trustee or recordkeeper when a plan loan should be "deemed" a distribution. If the bank does not receive "deeming" instructions from the plan fiduciary but has knowledge of delinquent loans, it should inform the plan fiduciary of the delinquent loans and periodically request instructions as to whether the delinquent loans should be "deemed" as distributions. Best practices for delinquent loans would be to insert language into the service agreement that delinquent loans are automatically deemed to be distributions within a certain time period if instructions to the contrary are not received.

The entire amount of the loan that is still outstanding becomes taxable if the participant does not cure the delinquent payments. The deemed distribution is reported on Form 1099-R and is subject to income tax as well as the 10 percent early distribution tax (unless an exception to the early distribution tax applies).

## Valuing Retirement Plan Assets

An accurate valuation of plan assets is essential to a plan's compliance with the IRC and ERISA. Most assets held by retirement plans are not difficult to value, such as mutual fund shares, certificates of deposit, and publicly traded stocks and bonds. Value determinations for some investments, such as real estate or stocks of privately held companies, are difficult.

The Annual Report Form 5500 on Schedule H requires the plan fiduciary to report the current value of plan assets and liabilities at the beginning and end of the plan year. The general investments of the plan are then broken out by type so that the plan's cash, U.S. Government securities, corporate debt, corporate stock, partnerships and joint ventures, real estate, mutual funds, insurance company contracts, collective funds, pooled separate accounts, master trusts, and all other assets are each accurately valued and listed.

In a defined benefit plan, valuation of the plan's assets is important as it determines whether the employer has adequately funded the plan. In an individual account plan, such as a 401(k) plan, the value of the plan's assets determines the value of the participant's account balance and thus the amount available for distribution or loans.

Under the IRC, ESOPs present special issues regarding valuation. An independent appraiser, upon the ESOP's purchase, must value nonpublicly traded employer securities, including preferred stock that is convertible into publicly traded common stock. The ESOP must value nonpublicly traded employer securities at least annually and upon special occurrences such as transactions with major shareholders. DOL regulations and case law impose a heavy burden on the fiduciary for determining the fair market value of the stock held by an ESOP. Because of the elevated risk associated with acting as trustee for an ESOP, bank fiduciaries must exercise care when determining whether appraisers are competent and independent and the appraisals appropriate.

Regardless of the types of retirement plans involved, banks should have sound, risk-based processes for periodic valuation of all assets, including those that are not widely traded. Assets that are difficult to value cost more to manage and may require independent valuations. The bank should determine who will pay these costs before the bank receives or acquires these assets. Sound, risk-based valuation processes for difficult-to-price assets will help reduce risk and will likely increase efficiency.

For more information, please see the "Unique and Hard-to-Value Assets" booklet of the *Comptroller's Handbook* as well as appendix B of this booklet, which addresses IRAs.

## Meeting Reporting Requirements

The federal government requires reporting and disclosure in the administration and operation of employee benefit plans to protect the interests of plan participants and beneficiaries. Disclosing reports to plan participants and their beneficiaries, and the filing of certain reports with the IRS and DOL, are required under both IRC and ERISA.

The plan fiduciary is responsible for these reporting and disclosure requirements. Plan fiduciaries may contract with service providers, including bank trustees, to assist them in meeting these requirements.

ERISA requires a plan fiduciary to file a comprehensive annual report, disclosing information relating to the plan's qualified status, financial condition, and operation. This annual report is Form 5500. Form 5500 is filed with the DOL, which forwards relevant information to the IRS and the Pension Benefit Guaranty Corporation. Form 5500 consists of three pension schedules and six general schedules. There are "small" plan rules regarding various parts of Form 5500 as well as "large" plan rules.

Schedule C is the service provider information form. Banks have the responsibility to provide plan fiduciaries with sufficient information for them to accurately complete a Schedule C form. The purpose of Schedule C is to inform the plan fiduciary and the DOL about compensation certain service providers receive (directly or indirectly) in connection with services rendered to the plan. Schedule C only requires reporting when a service provider's compensation is over $5,000. The definition of compensation includes money and any other thing of value (e.g., gifts, awards, trips). Schedule C also requires the reporting of compensation paid to service providers by any third party, in addition to compensation paid directly to the service provider. For example, fees received directly from the plan, as well as indirect soft-dollar benefits received from broker-dealers, are included on Schedule C.

Schedule C should also contain other fees such as 12b-1 fees and float income. In circumstances in which banks receive indirect compensation from multiple plans, the bank must have an allocation method for determining the indirect compensation for each individual plan. Plan fiduciaries should receive notice of the allocation method.

Under ERISA 103(a)(3)(A), a plan fiduciary must engage an independent qualified public accountant to examine financial statements of the plan and form an opinion as to whether the financial statements are presented fairly and in conformity with generally accepted accounting principles. The opinion of the independent qualified public accountant is then made a part of the plan's Form 5500. The only exception to this general rule is in ERISA 103(a)(3)(C) and its corresponding regulation at 29 CFR 2520.103-8. The exception is commonly referred to as the "limited scope audit exception." Under the limited scope audit exception, the independent qualified public accountant may rely on a financial statement prepared by a bank if the statement is certified. 29 CFR 2520.103-5 provides the requirements regarding the transmittal and contents of the certification.

Banks may also be required to prepare and file Form 1099-R for each person that has received a distribution of $10 or more from a pension plan. The 1099-R must show the name and address of the person, the aggregate amount of the distribution, and other information as required on the form. Banks must give a copy of the form to the individual receiving the distribution by January 31 and a copy to the IRS by the end of February.

Banks that provide products and services to employee benefit plans are required to include certain information regarding this line of business on Schedule RC-T to the FFIEC's 031 and 041, Consolidated Reports of Condition and Income (call report). Schedule RC-T requires a bank to report the market value and number of employee benefit accounts for which the bank serves as trustee or agent as well as the gross income and expenses generated from these accounts.

## Processing Transactions and Making Contingency Plans

The bank's information system must be capable of processing and reporting large volumes of many types of transactions and providing the fundamental accounting records and management reports necessary for the retirement plan products and services line of business. In addition to a primary trust accounting system, if the bank serves as a recordkeeper, there is a need for participant recordkeeping and client reporting systems designed specifically for the retirement plan market.

These mandatory retirement plan systems are complex and costly to obtain. In addition, ongoing changes in the retirement plan industry require a commitment to ongoing system upgrades and maintenance. The bank that wishes to provide products and services to retirement plans must be prepared to maintain appropriate systems, internal controls, and staffing.

Banks should also have strong controls reasonably designed to review and monitor the transmittal of funds based on instructions received. Controls should include a documented means, or method of customer confirmation, notification, or follow-up. Hackers may breach e-mail accounts or Internet connections and use them to commit fraud, so if banks accept instructions to withdraw or transfer funds by e-mail or other electronic means, there is increased risk and the need for strong controls. A method for verifying e-mail or online instructions sent by the plan sponsor (or designated party as determined and previously established by the plan sponsor) is a needed control. Controls should also include identifying and responding to "red flags," such as transfer requests that are out of the ordinary, transfer requests of funds to an unfamiliar, third-party account, or requests that indicate urgency or otherwise appear designed to deter verification of the transfer instructions. Useful guidance on customer account protection is in the Financial Industry Regulatory Authority's Regulatory Notice 12-05, "Verification of Emailed Instructions to Transmit or Withdraw Assets From Customer Accounts."

The bank must also make contingency plans for disruptions to data processing systems. A contingency plan, which is an extension of a bank's internal controls and physical security, specifies how the bank will continue operations after disruptions. If the bank relies on an outside servicer for the bulk of its data processing, it should take steps to determine whether the contingency plans of the servicer are adequate and whether the bank's own plans complement the servicer's. Comprehensive contingency planning policies and procedures for all business lines are a responsibility of the board of directors and senior management. For details regarding contingency planning, see the "Business Continuity Planning" booklet of the *FFIEC Information Technology (IT) Examination Handbook.*

## Escheatment

States may ask banks to report and remit unclaimed plan benefit payments as abandoned or unclaimed property under the state's escheat and unclaimed property statutes.

The DOL has determined, in AO 94-41A, that ERISA's broad preemption provision over all state laws that relate to employee benefit plans applies to state escheat and unclaimed property statutes. In DOL's view, the application of these state laws to an ongoing employee benefit plan "would directly affect the core functions of the plan by reducing, through escheatment, the amount of plan assets held in trust for the benefit of all participants and beneficiaries of the plan." Escheatment of ongoing employee benefit plan assets would be contrary to the interest of the plan and the participants and beneficiaries. The DOL has made it clear that state escheatment statutes do not apply to ongoing employee benefit plans.

In contrast with escheat issues regarding missing participants in an ongoing employee benefit plan, the DOL has issued different guidance regarding terminated retirement plans in FAB 2004-02. Plan fiduciaries may decide to escheat missing participants' account balances under a state's unclaimed property statute to complete the plan termination process. A fiduciary must first take certain steps, however, in an effort to locate a missing participant or beneficiary from the terminated plans. The DOL states that these steps involve only nominal expense and have a high potential for effectiveness in locating the missing or lost plan participant or beneficiary. Accordingly, fiduciaries must always use them, regardless of the size of the participant's account balance. These steps are to

- use certified mail.
- check related plan records.
- check with the designated plan beneficiary.
- use a letter forwarding service (U.S. Social Security Administration letter forwarding services).
- use Internet search tools.

FAB 2004-02 also states that the fiduciary should use certain steps, such as the use of commercial locator services and credit reporting agencies, if the fiduciary considers these actions are warranted by the size of the participant's account balance and the expenses involved in attempting to locate the missing participant. It goes on to state that reasonable expenses attendant to locating a missing participant may be charged to a participant's account, provided that the amount of the expenses allocated to the participant's account is reasonable and the method of allocation is consistent with the terms of the plan and the fiduciary's duties under ERISA.

Many banks have used the guidance in FAB 2004-02 in all situations involving missing or lost participants or beneficiaries. One change going forward is that, beginning on August 31, 2012, under IRS Revenue Procedure 2012-35, the IRS no longer forwards letters in an attempt to locate missing plan participants. The Social Security Administration has a letter-forwarding process, which is still in effect.

## Bundled Products and Services

Many banks offer a "one source" solution to the plan sponsor community, particularly for small businesses. This is the "bundled" retirement plan products and services approach, particularly for participant-directed, defined contribution plans such as 401(k)s. A bundled service package offers plan sponsors participant recordkeeping, investment, trustee, plan administration, and communication services. Banks that offer bundled services use either third-party vendors or their affiliates to provide some of the bundled services or keep all the operations in-house. These products and services often offer state-of-the-art participant and plan sponsor account access services through the Internet, voice response units, or call centers.

A typical bundled plan offers plan sponsors a mix of trustee and recordkeeping services, such as

- trustee services.
- plan adoption of the bank's prototype plans or volume submitter plans.
- selection and monitoring of investment funds.
- collection of mutual fund 12b-1 fees with appropriate fee offsets.
- certified trust statement.

- contribution determinations, earnings, and forfeiture allocations.
- maintenance and provision of participant statements.
- distribution, loan, and hardship withdrawal processing.
- provision and maintenance of prototype or volume submitter plan documents, summary plan descriptions, and administrative forms.
- Actual Deferral Percentage/Actual Contribution Percentage (ADP/ACP) testing, 415 limit testing, 401 coverage testing, and top-heavy testing.
- Form 5500 and Form 1099-R preparation.
- employee communication, education, and enrollment services.

Banks must have sufficient controls if processing the bundled products and services internally. If the bank is outsourcing, it needs controls to oversee the associated vendors or to review and monitor the information systems involved in the bundled arrangement.

## Participant Recordkeeping

Plan fiduciaries generally hire recordkeepers or TPAs to handle plan administration duties and to maintain participant account information. Recordkeepers or TPAs act at the direction of the plan fiduciary; they have no fiduciary status in regards to employee benefit plans. Recordkeepers or TPAs generally work closely with the plan trustee to make sure that plan level information reconciles with plan participant level information. The recordkeeper or TPA and the plan fiduciary have a detailed service agreement that specifies the duties of the recordkeeper or TPA.

Some of the more common functions of a recordkeeper or TPA are to

- advise the plan fiduciary on regulatory requirements regarding the administration of a plan.
- execute purchases and sales of investment options per participant elections.
- process participant loan and withdrawal requests.
- process benefit claims and payment of benefits at the direction of the plan fiduciary.
- assist the plan fiduciary with reporting and compliance testing.

Employers hire recordkeepers or TPAs to assist the employer and the trustee(s) because most employers and plan administrators are not familiar with the rules and regulations that govern employee benefit plans or do not have the human resources to handle all of the administrative and technical requirements of such plans. Recordkeepers or TPAs help determine who meets the plan's eligibility requirements, the amount of the contributions, and the extent of the participants' benefits. Recordkeepers or TPAs also assist in keeping employee benefit plans in compliance with the numerous employee benefit plan laws, particularly with regard to nondiscrimination tests.

Banks, or their affiliates, may act as recordkeepers or TPAs, or a non-affiliated third party may provide these services. The plan may contract directly with the third party, or the bank may contract with the third party. The liability to the bank varies accordingly.

The employer provides information on employee service and eligibility to the recordkeeper or TPA using the employee census. For each eligible participant, the recordkeeper or TPA maintains records of the amount contributed by the employer and the employee, before and after tax, the percent vested, the investments held in the participant's account, and the amount of any earnings. The recordkeeper or TPA accounts for changes in investment elections, calculates the maximum participant loan amount available, and processes distributions when a participant retires or terminates. The recordkeeper or TPA performs these duties at the direction of the plan administrator.

Recordkeepers or TPAs often perform discrimination tests. If the retirement plan is to maintain its preferred tax status, the plan must not discriminate in favor of highly compensated employees. There are a series of tests that ensure the plan does not favor highly compensated employees. The recordkeeper or TPA often determines who these highly compensated employees are, within the meaning of the IRC and plan provisions. Recordkeepers or TPAs may also perform various calculations to ensure that a plan conforms to tax requirements. These calculations may include determining whether the plan is "top heavy," performing IRC 415 calculations and 401(k) discrimination tests, and correcting failed ADP/ACP tests.

Plan fiduciaries are required to provide various disclosures to plan participants. They often outsource many of these duties to the recordkeeper or TPA. The most important of these are the summary plan description and the summary annual report. Recordkeepers or TPAs also file various IRS and DOL forms on behalf of the plan, including a request for an IRS Letter of Determination and annual DOL Form 5500 filings.

Employees who terminate their employment before becoming fully vested forfeit the unvested funds in their accounts. The disposition of forfeitures varies depending on the plan's provisions. Offsetting fees, reducing future employer contributions, or allocating to other participants are ways forfeitures are typically used.

Banks providing participant recordkeeping services should have sound transaction processing controls. The controls should ensure transactions are promptly and accurately posted. Transactions should be subject to routine internal control processes that ensure independent personnel

- balance all daily trades to participant records.
- balance aggregate totals to depository records, bank records, and participant records at least monthly.
- have processes to report aged, out-of-balance positions to management in a timely manner.

The bank and the recordkeeper or TPA must have systems that work together. When processing investment transactions and income, the bank aggregates the total buys and sells for each investment option and places trades for the aggregate amounts. The recordkeeping system takes the aggregated trades and allocates them to individual participant accounts. A critical control function is balancing the core trust accounting system to the participant recordkeeping system. Out-of-balance conditions should be aged and addressed.

# Examination Procedures

This booklet contains expanded procedures for examining specialized activities or specific products or services that warrant extra attention beyond the core assessment contained in the "Community Bank Supervision" and "Large Bank Supervision" booklets of the *Comptroller's Handbook*. Examiners determine which expanded procedures to use, if any, during examination planning or after drawing preliminary conclusions during the core assessment.

To determine the quantity and quality of management of a particular risk, examiners may select a sample of retirement plan accounts for review. If possible, include a variety of account types and bank capacities. Examiners and auditors (and others using this booklet) should ascertain in what capacity the bank is acting in regard to a retirement plan and in that capacity determine what products or services the bank has agreed to provide the plan. In general, the capacity and a description of the products and services the bank is providing the plan should be in the service agreement, trust agreement, or other plan documents. Trustees may have different duties or responsibilities for each retirement plan account as the trustees' duties and responsibilities are subject to negotiation and established by contract. The plan documents determine exactly what the bank's duties and responsibilities are for each retirement plan account.

## Scope

These procedures are designed to help examiners tailor examinations to certain banks and determine the scope of the retirement plan products and services examination. This determination should consider work performed by internal and external auditors, other independent risk control functions, and by other examiners in related areas. Examiners need to perform only those objectives and steps that are relevant to the scope of the examination as determined by the objectives in this section. Seldom is every objective or step of the expanded procedures necessary.

**Objective:** To determine the scope of the examination of retirement plan products and services and identify examination objectives and activities necessary to meet the needs of the supervisory strategy for the bank.

1. Review the following sources of information and note any previously identified problems related to retirement plan products and services that require follow up:

   - Supervisory strategy.
   - Previous reports of examination and work papers.
   - Internal and external audit reports and work papers.
   - Bank management's responses to previous reports of examination and audit reports.
   - Customer complaints and litigation.

2. Obtain the results of such reports as Schedule RC-T and the Uniform Bank Performance Reports.

3. Obtain and review policies, procedures, and reports bank management uses to supervise retirement plan products and services, including internal risk assessments and compliance reviews.

4. In discussions with bank management, determine whether there have been any significant changes (for example, in policies, processes, management [key and operational staff including portfolio managers and advisers], control systems [including changes to audit plan], products, volumes, markets, geographies, board and fiduciary committee structure and oversight, and operating systems) since the prior examination of retirement products and services.

5. Based on an analysis of information obtained in the previous steps, as well as input from the examiner-in-charge (EIC), determine the scope and objectives of the retirement plan products and services examination.

6. Select from the following examination procedures the necessary steps to meet examination objectives and the supervisory strategy.

# Quantity of Risk

## Conclusion: The quantity of each associated risk is (low, moderate, or high).

**Objective**: To determine the quantity of compliance risk associated with retirement plan products and services.

1. Analyze the types and level of policy exceptions, internal control deficiencies, and legal violations in relation to retirement plan products and services. Consider the level of compliance with

   - plan documents and other governing instruments.
   - ERISA, the IRC, and related DOL issuances.
   - 12 CFR 9 for national banks and 12 CFR 150 for federal savings associations.
   - other federal law.
   - bank's policies and operating procedures.
   - statutory exception from definition of "broker" in section 3(a)(4) of the Securities Exchange Act of 1934 and 12 CFR 218.721-723.
   - bank's BSA/AML/OFAC compliance program.

**Objective**: To determine the quantity of operational risk associated with retirement plan products and services.

2. Determine whether the bank has properly identified and measured the risks associated with the following:

   - Employer securities or real property.
   - Asset concentrations.
   - Nonpublicly traded assets and tangible assets.
   - Open brokerage windows in participant-directed, defined contribution plans.
   - Affiliated mutual funds.
   - Target date and life cycle collective funds.
   - Participant recordkeeping.

3. Analyze management information reports relating to transaction processing and reporting within the retirement plan products and services line of business. Consider the following structural factors:

   - Volume, type, and complexity of transactions, products, services, and investment vehicles offered through the bank.
   - Condition, security, capacity, and recoverability of systems.
   - Complexity and volume of conversions, integrations, and system changes.

- Development of new markets, products, services, technology, and delivery systems to maintain competitive position and gain strategic advantage.
- Volume and severity of operational, administrative, and accounting control exceptions and losses from fraud and operating errors.

**Objective**: To determine the level of strategic risk associated with retirement plan products and services.

4. Analyze the bank's strategic and business plans for retirement plan products and services.

   Consider the following factors:

   - Magnitude of change in projections related to income and earnings from retirement plan products and services.
   - Quantity and quality of management and staff in relation to current or projected retirement plan products and services.
   - Resources dedicated to training, improvements in technology, and marketing.
   - Past performance in offering new retirement products and services.
   - Risks associated with implementing innovative or unproven retirement plan products or services (including new delivery channels or technologies).

5. Assess the effect of external factors, including economic, industry, competitive, and market conditions.

6. Assess the effect of recent legislative, regulatory, accounting, and technological changes.

**Objective**: To determine the level of reputation risk associated with retirement plan products and services.

7. Analyze the types and volume of litigation and customer complaints by

   - discussing significant litigation and complaints with bank management.
   - determining the risk to capital and the appropriateness of corrective action and follow-up processes.

8. Review the most recently completed OCC examination activity of the bank's asset management operations by

   - discussing the findings and recommendations relating to retirement plan products and services with bank management.
   - determining whether management has taken corrective action to address previous concerns or to implement OCC recommendations.

Reach a conclusion on the types and quantity of risk from retirement plan products and services based on the findings of these and other related examination activities.

# Quality of Risk Management

---

## Conclusion: The quality of risk management is (strong, satisfactory, or weak).

---

The conclusion on risk management considers all risks associated with retirement plan products and services.

# Policies

Policies are statements of actions adopted by a bank to pursue certain objectives. Policies often set standards (on risk tolerances, for example) and should be consistent with the bank's underlying mission, values, and principles. A policy review should always be triggered when the bank's objectives or standards change.

**Objective:** To determine whether the board has adopted effective policies that are consistent with safe and sound banking practices that are appropriate to the size, nature, and scope of the bank's retirement plan products and services.

1. Evaluate relevant policies to determine whether they provide appropriate guidance for managing the bank's retirement plan products and services and are consistent with the bank's mission, values, and principles.

2. Determine whether policies establish risk limits or positions and delineate prudent actions to be taken if the limits are exceeded.

3. Verify that the board of directors or a designated committee periodically reviews and approves the bank's retirement plan products and services policies.

4. Verify that policies adequately address applicable law, including ERISA, 12 CFR 9 for national banks and 12 CFR 150 for federal savings associations, and the statutory exceptions to the definition of "broker" in the Securities Exchange Act of 1934, and Regulation R.

5. Determine whether the bank has appropriate policies to address potential prohibited transactions and conflicts of interest.

6. Verify that policies adequately address customer complaint resolution procedures.

7. Verify that policies include appropriate account acceptance and administration guidelines that address the following:

   - Pre-acceptance reviews.
   - Administration of accounts (including acceptance of contributions, payment of plan expenses, and distributions to participants and beneficiaries).

---

- Identifying, preventing, correcting, and reporting prohibited transactions.
- High-risk accounts (e.g., ESOPs) and high-risk assets (e.g., employer securities).
- Use of proprietary products in discretionary accounts.
- BSA/AML/OFAC compliance.
- Customer information privacy.
- Account closing.
- Client account statement guidelines.

# Processes

Processes are the procedures, programs, and practices that impose order on a bank's pursuit of its objectives. Processes define how daily activities are carried out. Effective processes are consistent with the underlying policies and are governed by appropriate checks and balances (such as internal controls).

**Objective:** To determine whether the bank has effective processes in place to define how the bank's retirement plan products and services are carried out.

1. Evaluate whether processes are effective, consistent with underlying polices, and effectively communicated to appropriate staff.

2. Determine whether appropriate internal controls are in place and functioning as designed. Consider

   - the effectiveness of periodic administrative account reviews for coding, governing instruments, list of those with distribution authority, and other administrative matters.
   - provision of investment advice or investment education materials.
   - avoiding or managing prohibited transactions.
   - for directed trustee accounts - documentation regarding whether directions are in accordance with the plan and not contrary to ERISA.
   - compliance with section 3(a)(4) of Securities Exchange Act of 1934 and 12 CFR 218.721-723 (Regulation R).
   - documentation and handling of account complaints and litigation.
   - disclosure to plan fiduciaries and reporting of compensation such as 12b-1, subtransfer, and other fees from mutual funds; use of float; overdrafts; sweep fees; and gains from the correction of trading errors.
   - timeliness of employer and employee contributions.
   - payment of plan expenses.
   - processing of plan loans.
   - valuation of plan assets.
   - accuracy of information for Form 5500 reporting.
   - escheatment provisions.
   - accuracy of account statements.

3. Determine whether appropriate internal controls are in place and functioning as designed regarding retirement plan account acceptance. Consider

   - pre-acceptance reviews.
   - use of account checklists.
   - proper deposit and continued accounting of plan assets.
   - review for conflicts of interest.
   - compliance with BSA/AML/OFAC requirements.

4. Determine whether appropriate internal controls are in place and functioning as designed for retirement plan investments. Consider

   - existence of investment policy statement.
   - investment review of plan assets for discretionary accounts.
   - proxy voting.
   - accurate valuation of plan assets particularly for unique and hard to value assets.
   - plan's use of employer securities.
   - cross-trades.
   - use of bank's deposit products.
   - use of bank's collective investment funds.

5. Determine whether appropriate internal controls are in place and functioning as designed for retirement plan distributions. Consider

   - authorization of distributions.
   - processing lump sum or periodic participant distributions.
   - hardship or other in-service withdrawals.
   - QDRO distributions.
   - distribution at termination of employment.
   - early withdrawals.
   - rollover distributions.
   - proper federal tax withholding.
   - appropriate OFAC checks.

6. Determine whether appropriate internal controls are in place and functioning as designed for operational functions, using as references any independent tests of the control structure, such as internal or external audits. Consider

   - data input and balancing functions.
   - participant's use of voice response units or Internet to provide transaction instructions.
   - appropriate authorization to release funds or assets.
   - logical (ID and password) access to automated systems.
   - high-risk processes (e.g., participant recordkeeping, payment of plan expenses, plan contributions, participant distributions, and tax reporting).

- data security.
- independent reconcilement.
- exception monitoring.

7. If the bank (or an affiliate) is a recordkeeper, determine whether the bank has effective procedures in place to balance the recordkeeping system to the core trust accounting system. Procedures should include the following:

- Reconciling between the two systems.
- Verifying that transactions, pricing, and other information received through system interfaces are processed timely and accurately.
- Verifying that transactions, such as changes to investment allocations, contribution levels, and pricing updates received through system interfaces or direct input are processed timely. This often involves reviewing reports reflecting voice response unit or Internet activity and rejects from daily processing.
- Evaluating procedures for resolution of reconciling differences. Outstanding items should be aged and escalated.
- Ensuring that there is a process for balancing participant statements to core accounting statements.

# Personnel

Personnel are the bank staff and managers who execute or oversee processes. Personnel should be qualified and competent and should perform appropriately. They should understand the bank's mission, values, principles, policies, and processes. Banks should design compensation programs to attract, develop, and retain qualified personnel. In addition, compensation programs should be structured in a manner that encourages strong risk management practices.

**Objective**: To determine management's ability to supervise retirement plan products and services in a safe and sound manner.

1. Given the scope and complexity of the bank's retirement plan products and services, assess the management structure and staffing. Consider

- training.
- the number of accounts administrative personnel are responsible for.
- whether reporting lines encourage open communication and limit the chances of conflicts of interest.
- level of staff turnover.
- capability and authority to address identified deficiencies.
- responsiveness to regulatory, accounting, industry, and technological changes.
- experience of management and staff based on the complexity of the bank's retirement plan products and services.
- adequacy of staffing levels.

2. Assess performance management and compensation programs. Consider whether these programs measure and reward performance that aligns with the bank's strategic objectives and risk appetite.

   If the bank offers incentive compensation programs, ensure that they are consistent with OCC Bulletin 2010-24, "Incentive Compensation: Interagency Guidance on Sound Incentive Compensation Policies," including compliance with its three key principles: (1) provide employees with incentives that appropriately balance risk and reward; (2) be compatible with effective controls and risk management; and (3) be supported by strong corporate governance, including active and effective oversight by the bank's board of directors.

## Control Systems

Control systems are the functions (such as internal and external audits, risk review, and quality assurance) and information systems that bank managers use to measure performance, make decisions about risk, and assess the effectiveness of processes. Control functions should have clear reporting lines, adequate resources, and appropriate authority. Management information systems should provide timely, accurate, and relevant feedback.

**Objective:** To determine whether the bank has systems in place to provide accurate and timely assessments of the risks associated with its retirement plan products and services.

1. Assess the scope, frequency, effectiveness, and independence of the internal and external audits of the bank's retirement plan products and services. Consider

   - frequency and scope of audits performed, including whether all significant activities and controls are covered.
   - level of the audit staff's expertise in retirement plan products and services.
   - quality of audit reports and supporting work papers.
   - board and senior management information reports, escalation plans, and actions taken in response to deficiencies.

2. Determine whether the management information systems provide timely, accurate, and useful information to evaluate risk levels and trends in the bank's retirement plan products and services. Consider

   - whether the management information system is timely, accurate, and useful for measuring performance of administrative and operational functions.
   - management's use of earnings reports, risk assessments, audit reports, compliance reports, committee reports, and litigation reports.
   - whether the management information system is timely, accurate, and useful for identifying and managing risk in the bank's retirement plan products and services.

3. Evaluate fiduciary committee structures, responsibilities, and performance.

4. Evaluate the effectiveness of monitoring systems to identify, measure, and track exceptions to policies and procedures.

5. When the bank contracts with third parties (including affiliates) to provide retirement plan products and services, determine the adequacy of the bank's selection and monitoring processes. Refer to OCC Bulletin 2013-29, "Third-Party Relationships: Risk Management Guidance," for guidance. For data-processing services, determine whether the board or a designated committee reviews the vendor's financial information annually. Refer to the "Outsourcing Technology Services" booklet of the *FFIEC IT Examination Handbook* for guidance. Consider the bank's processes for

   • vendor due diligence reviews.
   • contract negotiations and approvals.
   • vendor monitoring, including the frequency and quality of information reviewed.
   • identifying personnel to serve as the point of contact with the vendor and to conduct ongoing monitoring.

6. Evaluate the effectiveness of formal compliance and risk management functions. Consider

   • formal and informal structures.
   • reporting lines—whether independent or within the line of business.
   • quality of risk assessment (identification of high-risk processes).
   • control self-assessments.
   • reporting procedures.
   • follow-up on weaknesses identified by compliance and risk management reviews, audits, regulatory examinations, etc.
   • litigation and complaint processes.
   • training and expertise in the retirement services area.

# Conclusions

---

## Conclusion: The aggregate level of each risk is (low, moderate, or high). The direction of each risk is (increasing, stable, or decreasing).

---

**Objective:** To determine, document, and communicate overall findings and conclusions regarding the examination of retirement plan products and services.

1. Determine preliminary examination findings and conclusions and discuss with the EIC, including

   - quantity of associated risks.
   - quality of risk management.
   - aggregate level and direction of associated risks.
   - the overall risk in retirement plan products and services.
   - violations and other concerns.
   - potential violations of ERISA that may require referral to the DOL, pursuant to OCC Bulletin 2006-24, "Interagency Agreement on ERISA Referrals: Information Sharing Between the FFIEC Agencies and the DOL."

| Summary of Risks Associated With Retirement Plan Products and Services | | | | |
|---|---|---|---|---|
| Risk category | Quantity of risk<br><br>(Low, moderate, high) | Quality of risk management<br><br>(Weak, satisfactory, strong) | Aggregate level of risk<br><br>(Low, moderate, high) | Direction of risk<br><br>(Increasing, stable, decreasing) |
| Operational | | | | |
| Compliance | | | | |
| Strategic | | | | |
| Reputation | | | | |

2. Discuss examination findings with the asset management EIC and adjust findings and recommendations as needed. Contact the supervisory office before the exit meeting with management if the retirement plan products and services area exhibits significant weaknesses or concerns, such as the following:

   - Area is less than satisfactory.
   - Bank's policies, procedures, or controls have not proven effective and require strengthening.
   - Uniform Interagency Trust Rating System (UITRS) compliance assessment shows significant weaknesses.
   - Exam findings are likely to contribute to a UITRS composite rating of 3 or worse.

---

- Level of risk is moderate and increasing because of retirement plan products and services.
- Level of any risk is high because of retirement plan products and services.

3. Discuss examination findings with bank management, including violations, recommendations, and conclusions about risks and risk management practices. If necessary, obtain commitments for corrective action.

4. Compose conclusion comments, highlighting any issues that should be included in the report of examination. If necessary, compose a Matters Requiring Attention.

5. Update the OCC's information system and any applicable report of examination schedules or tables.

6. Write a memorandum specifically setting out what the OCC should do in the future to effectively supervise retirement plan products and services, including time periods, staffing, and workdays required. Provide memorandum to asset management EIC for review, approval, and submission to EIC.

7. Update, organize, and reference work papers in accordance with OCC policy.

8. Ensure any paper or electronic media that contain sensitive bank or customer information are appropriately disposed of or secured.

# Appendixes

## Appendix A: Types of Retirement Plans

Congress periodically changes the applicable dollar amounts, percentages, and employee age requirements for the various retirement plans discussed in this section through amendments to the IRC and ERISA.

### Employee Benefit Pension Plans

An employee pension benefit plan is any plan, fund, or program that is established or maintained by an employer or employee organization that provides retirement income to employees.

Employee pension benefit plans can be either qualified or nonqualified. A qualified plan is one that "qualifies" for special tax treatment under IRC 401(a). Corporations, other business entities, and self-employed persons can establish qualified retirement plans.

Nonqualified plans defer compensation or otherwise provide benefits payable at retirement or termination of employment but do not qualify for favorable tax treatment. Generally, nonqualified plans include executive or incentive compensation arrangements.

To qualify for favorable tax treatment, a retirement plan must meet certain standards, including

- adequate, nondiscriminatory coverage of employees.
- minimum vesting requirements.
- minimum distribution requirements.
- nondiscriminatory contributions and benefit accruals.

There are two categories of qualified retirement plans: defined benefit or defined contribution. There are a wide variety of plans that fall under these broad categories. The one thing they have in common is that they must meet the strict standards set by the IRC to maintain their qualified status.

### Master and Prototype Plans

When a bank provides retirement plan services to a defined benefit or defined contribution plan, the bank's file generally includes documents that specify whether the retirement plan is maintained as a "master" or "prototype" plan. The IRS pre-approves these plans, which are then made available for employers to adopt.

Under a master plan, the sponsoring organization establishes a single funding medium (e.g., trust account) for joint use by all adopting employers. The employer executes an adoption agreement to establish a plan using the master plan document. The sponsoring organization files the plan document form, the adoption agreement, and the trust agreement with the IRS. The sponsor then asks for an opinion that the master plan is acceptable to the IRS as a qualified plan and meets all the latest IRS 401(a) requirements.

A master plan consists of three parts:

1. A basic plan document, which is identical for all the employers that adopt the plan.
2. An adoption agreement, which generally contains options that an employer may select that relate to eligibility, vesting, and contribution or benefit levels.
3. A trust agreement under which all participating plan investments are held.

A prototype plan is similar to a master plan except that the sponsoring organization establishes a separate funding medium for each adopting employer. Prototype plans are much more prevalent in the retirement plan services industry than master plans. In addition to financial institutions, law firms and accounting firms are common sponsors of prototype plans.

Master or prototype plans may be standardized or non-standardized. The IRS approves a standardized plan. An employer that adopts a standardized defined contribution (DC) plan may generally rely on the sponsoring organization's IRS opinion letter and does not need to secure a separate determination letter. The IRS pre-approves non-standardized plans but an adopting employer may want to apply for approval of an individual plan adoption with the IRS.

## Defined Benefit Pension Plans

These plans guarantee a specific or determinable benefit to participants at normal retirement age and require the sponsoring employer to contribute over a period of years whatever amounts are necessary to fund these benefits. A formula establishes eligibility for retirement based upon factors such as the employee's age and years of service. Because a defined benefit plan promises a certain benefit to an employee at his or her retirement, the employer is responsible for contributing to the plan the amount of funds necessary to pay benefits when they are due. These plans retain an actuary to determine what dollar level of contribution is necessary from the employer. An employer can reduce its required contributions if the investments perform better than the actuary has assumed, or if salaries do not increase as expected. Conversely, if the investments do not perform as well as the actuary assumes, or if employee salaries increase faster than assumed, the employer must increase its contributions to make up the difference. Funding policies for defined benefit plans are complex because they must address the issue of liabilities (both accumulated and projected) in the form of benefit payments and determine how to fund these liabilities through contributions and the expected return on investment of these funds.

While a sponsoring employer may decide to freeze some or all of the benefits associated with its defined benefit plan, ensuring compliance with ERISA's requirements (e.g., notices, distributions, nondiscrimination rules, and benefit eligibility) remains an ongoing issue for the bank that serves in a fiduciary capacity for that frozen plan.

ERISA created the PBGC to provide a federal insurance program that insures participants against the loss of benefits. In certain circumstances, such as when the employer becomes insolvent before contributing sufficient amounts to fund accrued benefits under the plan, the PBGC steps in and pays participants' pension benefits up to certain levels. The plan sponsor pays premiums to the PBGC on a per-participant, per-year basis for this coverage. With minor exceptions, all defined benefit plans covered by ERISA are also covered by the PBGC.

**Cash Balance Plans**

Cash balance plans are a form of defined benefit plan. They exhibit features of both defined benefit and defined contribution plans. Unlike traditional defined benefit plans, in which an employee's benefit is expressed by a formula and can be difficult to track during the employee's working career, in a cash balance plan the employee's benefit is expressed as hypothetical "pay credits" and "interest credits" to the cash account. Cash balance plans provide higher benefits for younger employees and lower benefits for older employees, in contrast with defined benefit plans. This is because employer accruals under a typical cash balance plan remain relatively level, increasing only slightly toward the end of an employee's career. Employer accruals under a traditional defined benefit pension plan begin relatively low but increase sharply as an employee approaches retirement.

## Defined Contribution Pension Plans

These plans do not promise a specific benefit. Each participant has an individual account under the plan and is entitled only to the amount in his or her account at retirement age. Cumulative net contributions, distributions, expenses, and gains or losses associated with the participant's account determine the amount of an employee's benefit. The employer makes contributions based on a formula established in the plan such as a percentage of profits of the company, the salary of a participant, or any number of other factors. Under some plans, the participant may also elect to make contributions to the plan out of his or her own salary. The PBGC does not insure defined contribution plans. There are several types of defined contribution plans, as described in the following paragraphs.

**Profit-Sharing Plans**

In a profit-sharing plan (a type of defined contribution plan), each year the employer contributes to the plan an amount determined at the employer's discretion, or based on a formula in the plan. They typically allocate the contribution proportionately according to the compensation paid to each participant for the year. The company need not make a profit to contribute to the plan, even though the plans are called "profit sharing." Employer securities are often among the plan's assets.

**401(k) Plans**

These are individual account defined contribution plans. The employee may direct the employer to contribute part of the employee's salary to his or her account. Known as "elective deferral contributions," these amounts are usually a percentage of compensation.

Elective contributions can be made on a pretax basis or after-tax basis, depending on the plan terms. They are subject to certain limits. Pretax contributions are excluded from the employee's gross income for the year in which they are made, and they are not subject to taxation until distributed. In addition to employee deferral contributions, the employer may make matching contributions. A formula determines the employer's contribution (e.g., the employer contributes $1 for each $1 contributed by the employee, to a maximum of 3 percent of salary). Employer contributions may be in cash or in company stock, as provided in the plan document.

In many of these plans, employees can choose to place their plan account assets into several investment vehicles preselected by the plan sponsor. Like profit-sharing plans, 401(k) plans may include employer stock as one of the investment options.

**Money Purchase Pension Plans**

These plans require an employer to contribute a specific percentage of eligible employees' compensation to the plan each year, which makes the age and length of service of the participant irrelevant for both contribution and allocation purposes. The obligation to fund the plan makes money purchase pension plans (MPPP) different from most profit-sharing plans. Employers may pay a penalty if they do not make required contributions. The advantage offered by MPPPs is that an employer, such as a small business, may contribute the lesser of 25 percent of compensation or $51,000 (for 2013), to an employee's MPPP account. These contributions are tax deductible by the employer and accumulate on a tax-deferred basis until withdrawn at retirement.

**Target Benefit Plans**

These are individual account plans that are a hybrid of a money purchase plan and a defined benefit plan. They provide a "targeted" benefit upon retirement. They are like defined benefit plans in that the employer makes contributions to each participant account through a defined benefit formula calculated by an actuary. They are like typical defined contribution plans in that there are no guarantees that there will be payment of the targeted benefit at retirement. If the earnings of the fund differ from those assumed, it increases or decreases the benefits payable to the participant, instead of causing an increase or decrease in employer contributions. In this regard, a target benefit plan operates much like an MPPP. The difference is that with an MPPP, contributions for identically compensated employees are the same even though their ages differ; in a target benefit plan, age is one of the factors that determine the size of the contributions.

**Employee Stock Ownership Plans**

ESOPs invest "primarily" in publicly traded common stock of the employer. If the employer has no publicly traded common stock, the ESOP may invest in common stock with voting power and dividend rights that are equal to or greater than that of any class of the employer's common stock. The ESOP may invest in preferred stock under certain conditions. In connection with the purchase by the ESOP, an independent appraiser must value nonpublicly traded employer securities, including preferred stock that is convertible into publicly traded common stock. The ESOP must value nonpublicly traded employer securities at least annually and upon special occurrences such as transactions with major shareholders. DOL regulations and case law have imposed a heavy burden on the fiduciary to be responsible for determining the fair market value of the stock held by an ESOP. Because of the elevated risk associated with acting as trustee for an ESOP, bank fiduciaries must exercise care when determining whether appraisers are competent and independent, and the appraisals appropriate.

In a leveraged ESOP, the ESOP borrows money from the bank (which may also be the trustee bank) or other qualified lender and uses the proceeds of the loan to purchase employer stock. The company usually guarantees repayment of the loan. There are specific exemptions from ERISA's prohibited transaction rules for loans to leveraged ESOPs. The ESOP holds the employer stock in a suspense account as the primary or sole asset of the ESOP. The employer is obligated to make annual contributions to the ESOP. The ESOP uses the annual employer contributions to make periodic principal and interest payments on the loan, pursuant to the loan agreement between the ESOP trustee and the lender. When the ESOP makes loan repayments, stock is released from the suspense account to the accounts of ESOP participants. The IRC and ERISA permit qualified retirement plans other than ESOPs to borrow money. Only ESOPs can borrow money using the credit or guarantees of the plan sponsor.

Regardless of how the plan acquires stock, company contributions to the trust are tax-deductible, within certain IRC limits. The trust allocates its shares to individual employee accounts. The ESOP plan document specifies whether an employee leaving the company receives the vested balance in stock or cash. If it is in stock, the company must agree to buy it back from the employee at its fair market value (unless there is a public market for the shares).

In private companies, employees must be able to vote their allocated shares on major issues, such as closing a plan or relocating employees. In public companies, employees must be able to vote on all issues.

**403(b) Plans**

These are plans established under IRC 403(b) for certain employees of public schools, tax-exempt organizations, and certain ministers. These plans may be referred to as a "tax-sheltered annuity plan," although, since 1974, the plans are no longer restricted to an annuity form. The features of a 403(b) plan are very similar to those of a 401(k) plan. Employees may make salary deferral contributions that are subject to maximum contribution rates. Like the 401(k)s, pre-tax contributions and earnings remain tax free until withdrawn.

Individual accounts in a 403(b) plan can be any of the following types:

- An annuity contract, which is provided through an insurance company.
- A custodial account, which is invested in mutual funds.
- A retirement income account set up for church employees.

## 457 Plans

These are plans established under IRC 457 for employees of state and local governments or tax-exempt organizations. A 457 plan is similar to a 401(k) plan except that there are generally no employer matching contributions. Also, the IRS does not consider it a qualified retirement plan (although many of the features of qualified retirement plans apply to governmental 457 plans and ERISA guidelines are often incorporated by reference in the plan documents). Participants can defer some of their annual income (up to an annual limit) and contributions and earnings are tax-deferred until withdrawal.

The 457(b) plan assets of tax-exempt employers are subject to the claims of the employer's creditors, but the plans sponsored by governmental entities are not. Plan distributions may occur at retirement, on separation from employment, as the result of an unforeseeable emergency, or at death. Distributions are subject to immediate taxation at ordinary income tax rates.

## Keogh (HR-10) Plans

These are qualified retirement plans established by the Self-Employed Individuals Tax Retirement Act of 1962, otherwise known as the Keogh Act, or HR-10. Self-employed persons, partnerships, or owners of unincorporated businesses may set up Keogh plans. A Keogh plan may be a defined contribution plan or a defined benefit plan. Keogh plans may authorize plan loans. Contributions and all earnings accumulate free of tax until withdrawn, generally at retirement. Under normal circumstances, withdrawals before age 59½ are subject to a 10 percent distribution penalty in addition to ordinary income tax, however, distributions are eligible for transfer to an IRA.

## Savings Incentive Match Plan for Employees (SIMPLE plan)

Employers with 100 or fewer employees receiving at least $5,000 in compensation from the employer in the preceding year may adopt a simplified retirement plan, the SIMPLE plan, if they do not currently maintain another plan. The plan allows employees to make elective contributions up to a certain amount per year and requires employers to make matching contributions. Assets in the account are not taxed until they are distributed to an employee, and an employer may generally deduct contributions to the employee's accounts. A primary advantage of the SIMPLE plan is that it is not subject to the nondiscrimination rules (including top-heavy provisions) or other complex requirements applicable to qualified plans. In addition, the reporting requirements that normally apply to plans under ERISA are significantly relaxed for SIMPLE plans. SIMPLE plans may be structured as an IRA or as a 401(k) qualified cash or deferred arrangement.

## Simplified Employee Pension Plans

These are IRA based plans defined in IRC 408(k). A SEP allows a small employer to avoid the complex administration and expense of qualified retirement plans when establishing a retirement plan for employees. Under a SEP, an employer may contribute to IRAs established in each employee's name (SEP-IRAs). An employer's contributions to a SEP are discretionary and employee vesting is immediate. Employees may withdraw or transfer funds at any time. Because these accounts are IRAs, the amounts held in an SEP-IRA are subject to all IRS rules regarding transfer, withdrawal, and taxation.

## Taft–Hartley Plans

Many companies maintain qualified retirement plans under collective bargaining agreements for those union workers who typically move from one employer to the next as specific jobs start and finish. Often a retirement plan negotiated by a union is set up on an industry-wide basis. In multi-employer plans, two or more unrelated employers may participate in the plan under a collective bargaining agreement. These plans are very common in certain industries, such as construction, transportation, and mining. The main difference between these plans and other qualified plans is that a multi-employer plan is managed by a board of trustees composed of both union and employer representatives. A Taft–Hartley plan may provide union members with defined benefit or defined contribution benefits, including 401k options, as well as health and welfare benefits.

# Appendix B: Individual Retirement Accounts

This section addresses the administration of IRAs. IRAs are personal retirement plans created or organized in the United States for the exclusive benefit of an individual. The plan must be in the form of a trust or custodial account, and must satisfy all the requirements outlined in IRC 408 and related tax regulations. The laws and regulations have changed numerous times over the years, so it is always best to check the most recent version of IRC 408, as well as related regulations, to see if IRAs held at the bank meet the conditions specified in IRC 408 and associated regulations. The DOL generally does not have jurisdiction over nonemployer-sponsored IRAs as they do not fall under title I of ERISA. The IRS has jurisdiction over these accounts. The DOL, however, has the authority to issue interpretations of IRC 4975 that involve prohibited IRA transactions. There are some PTEs issued jointly by the DOL and the IRS, involving IRAs and AOs issued by the DOL, discussed in this section. SEP-IRAs established by an employer under IRC 408(k) may be subject to ERISA 404 and 406, covering fiduciary responsibility and prohibited transactions.

IRAs have several tax advantages, including the following:

- Contributions made to an IRA may be fully or partially deductible, depending on which type of IRA is established and on the circumstances of the individual.
- Until distribution, funds held within the IRA (including earnings and gains) are not taxed. In some cases, there is no tax liability if the distribution is in accordance with the rules.

Many banks offer IRA services to their customers. Banks provide these services in one of two capacities, "trustee" or "custodian." To determine whether the bank is serving as trustee or custodian of an IRA, look at the form used to establish the IRA. For example, the top line of Form 5305, an IRS Form that is a model trust agreement, states "Traditional Individual Retirement Trust Account." The top line of Form 5305-A, another IRS Form that is a model custodian account, states "Traditional Individual Retirement Custodial Account." The language in the two forms is identical, except one uses the term "trustee" and the other uses the term "custodian."

Banks do not need fiduciary powers when acting as a custodian to an IRA or to any other type of custodial account. For purposes of 12 CFR 9 for national banks and 12 CFR 150 for federal savings associations, however, the bank is a fiduciary with respect to an IRA if the bank is named trustee, exercises investment discretion, or otherwise acts in a "fiduciary capacity" as defined in 12 CFR 9.2(e) for national banks and 12 CFR 150.30 for federal savings associations. Banks are required to have fiduciary powers to serve as a trustee for an IRA. Federal savings associations are not required to have fiduciary powers to serve as a trustee for an IRA (12 CFR 150.580)

Banks with fiduciary powers often provide investment advice or investment management to IRA owners, particularly for rollover IRAs. A rollover IRA is established when a customer withdraws cash or other assets from a retirement plan and contributes those assets within 60 days to another eligible retirement plan (such as an IRA). This often happens when an individual retires with a 401(k), 403(b), or governmental 457 retirement plan, and chooses or is required to transfer the assets of that plan into an IRA. Many financial experts encourage retirees to rollover in order to gain maximum control over their retirement funds, particularly when the company retirement plan has limited investment choices or high fees.

## Types of IRAs

There are two primary types of nonemployer-sponsored IRAs: traditional IRAs and Roth IRAs. In traditional IRAs, individuals make contributions, which may or may not be tax deductible. Distributions are generally taxable income to the recipient. Contributions to Roth IRAs are on an after-tax basis, and qualified distributions are generally tax free. Traditional IRAs are subject to various minimum distribution rules when the owner attains age 70½ or dies. There are no minimum distribution rules for Roth IRAs while the owner is alive. With both types of IRAs there are various eligibility and contribution limits.

Traditional IRAs are available to those under age 70½ who have employment compensation (i.e., wages). Nonworking spouses are also eligible to contribute to traditional IRAs. Contributions to traditional IRAs are only fully tax deductible to the extent that employees and any nonworking spouses are not eligible for retirement plans from the employees' employers. If they are eligible for a retirement plan, the deductibility of an IRA is subject to an income test.

Roth IRAs were created in 1998. The primary difference between a Roth IRA and most traditional IRAs is that contributions to a Roth IRA are not tax deductible and eligibility is restricted to those whose earned income, as measured by their adjusted gross income (AGI). Roth IRAs have several benefits, such as nontaxable earnings (when distributed in a qualified distribution) and no lifetime required minimum distributions, even at age 70½.

Traditional IRA owners may choose to convert their traditional IRA into a Roth IRA. There are no eligibility requirements to convert IRAs. Some factors that traditional IRA owners may consider when deciding to convert are the owner's current tax rate, the owner's predicted tax rate at the time of distribution, and the owner's current ability or desire to pay the taxes. The larger the percentage of nondeductible contributions contained in a traditional IRA, the more desirable it is to convert to a Roth IRA, because there are no owed taxes on the conversion of nondeductible contributions. Only the earnings and the return of deductible contributions are subject to income tax upon conversion.

## Contribution Limits

Annual contributions to traditional IRAs are generally tax deductible for the owner. This is not tax avoidance; it is only a deferral as distributions are taxable income to the owner or beneficiary. If the owner is not eligible for an employer-sponsored qualified retirement plan, contributions are always deductible. There are certain income limits (subject to inflation adjustment), if the owner is eligible for a qualified plan. For Roth IRAs, contributions are never deductible. There are limits on the amount of annual income the owner may have and, if he or she exceeds this amount, he or she may be limited or precluded from making a contribution. Additionally, there are annual contribution limits based on the owner's age for all forms of IRAs. Because these various limits are adjusted based on inflation, refer to current IRS guidance for the specific limits in any given year. The contribution limitations apply to all IRAs an individual may possess, regardless of the type. An individual may not exceed the total annual limit but may apportion contributions among two or more accounts.

Generally, contributions to IRAs must be in cash. The only exception is for rollovers from qualified plans or other IRAs. Any other contribution of property would constitute a prohibited transaction.

## Rollovers

A rollover is a tax-free distribution to the account holder of cash or other assets from one retirement plan that is immediately contributed to another retirement plan. Both traditional and Roth IRAs may accept rollovers from qualified employee benefit retirement plans, such as a 401(k) plan, a 403(b), or governmental 457 plan. With traditional IRAs, this is generally a tax-free event; however, the owner is subject to taxation during the year of the rollover when the rollover goes into a Roth IRA.

The trustee of the qualified plan can issue funds directly to an IRA or can issue the funds to the participant, who then has 60 days to place them in the rollover IRA. If the latter option is used, the qualified plan must withhold 20 percent of the distribution for income taxes. The account holder would then have to obtain these funds from a different source to avoid some of the distribution being taxable.

## Distributions

Distributions from traditional IRAs are taxable events to the recipient. Additionally, if the owner takes distributions before attaining the age of 59½, these distributions are generally subject to a 10 percent penalty tax. There are several exceptions to the penalty tax that may be applicable. Again, these rules have historically been subject to frequent adjustments and modifications, so refer to current IRS guidance for the latest rules.

For traditional IRAs, the owner must begin taking required minimum distributions on an annual basis by April 1 of the year following the year he or she turns 70½. This is the required minimum distribution beginning date. If there are no distributions, or the distributions are not large enough, a 50 percent excise tax on the amount not distributed may be imposed. The individual's life expectancy, as determined by IRS tables, and the value of the account as of December 31 of the preceding year, determine the required minimum distribution.

In the event the owner dies before the required beginning date, the rules vary based on whether the beneficiary is the IRA owner's spouse or someone else designated by the owner or specified in the IRA agreement.

If the beneficiary is the IRA owner's spouse, the spouse has the option of leaving the funds in the deceased spouse's IRA and taking distributions based on the decedent's required beginning date, or treating the IRA as his or her own IRA and taking distributions based on his or her own required beginning date.

If there is a stated beneficiary in the IRA agreement, distribution calculations are based on the beneficiaries' life expectancy in the year of the owner's death, reduced by one for each year after the year of death. Distributions generally begin in the year following the owner's death.

If there is no beneficiary designation, or if an estate or trust is the designated beneficiary, the entire account must be distributed by December 31 of the fifth year following the owner's death.

If death occurs after the owner's required beginning date, distributions are made over the longer of the beneficiary's life expectancy or the life expectancy of the decedent at the time of death, again reduced by one for each year after the year of death.

For Roth IRAs, the owner is never required to take a distribution but beneficiaries are subject to the distribution rules.

## Investments

The trustee or custodian of any IRA may act in a directed capacity, or may have investment responsibilities. In order for a trustee or custodian that is subject to OCC supervision to have investment authority, the trustee or custodian must have fiduciary powers. In the event the bank has investment responsibilities for the account, the IRA agreement or a second ancillary agreement should clearly define the duties and responsibilities of both the bank and the account holder. For those accounts where the institution has investment responsibility, the OCC fiduciary regulations in 12 CFR 9 for national banks and 12 CFR 150 for federal savings associations apply.

Generally, an IRA can hold assets similar to those held by traditional trusts, but there are exceptions. Under IRC 408(a)(3), IRAs may not hold life insurance or most collectibles. There is an exception in IRC 408(m)(3) for bullion coins issued by the United States or any state therein.

It is critical that all IRA investments be registered or titled in the name of the IRA or a nominee name for the IRA trustee or custodian. In addition, the IRA trustee or custodian must take possession of the ownership evidence of that property. At the closing of a purchase of property, for example, the representative of the IRA trustee or custodian should be present, sign the necessary documents, and present a check drawn from the IRA. If the IRA owner were to purchase the property and have the property titled in his or her name and then put the investment into his or her IRA, a prohibited transaction would occur. The IRA owner would be selling the investment to his or her IRA.

If a bank is a trustee of an IRA but the IRA owner is directing the bank as to the investment of the IRA assets, then the bank must ensure that the IRA owner receives the disclosures required under the Interagency Statement on Retail Sales of Nondeposit Investment Products. The required disclosures should be in writing and presented in a clear and concise manner. The disclosures, at a minimum, should specify that the IRA investments are not insured by the Federal Deposit Insurance Corporation; not a deposit or other obligation of, or guaranteed by, the bank; and subject to investment risks, including possible loss of the principal amount invested.

The trustee or custodian is free to impose more restrictive investment rules under its policies and can substantially limit the types of assets the account can hold as investments. Banks, whether they are trustee or custodian of the IRA, have a responsibility to provide a fair market value of the IRA assets on Form 5498, which is filed annually with the IRS (see discussion of Form 5498 in the "Reporting and Disclosure Requirements" section of this booklet). The IRA should have adequate liquid assets to pay for an appraisal of investments, such as real estate, private placement limited partnerships, and closely held stocks; or the bank's fee should be high enough to absorb these costs. For more information, banks and examiners should refer to the "Unique and Hard-to-Value Assets" booklet of the *Comptroller's Handbook.*

Examiners should note that, although IRA account assets are permitted under IRC 408(a)(5) and the OCC's rules at 12 CFR 9.18 to be invested in bank collective investment funds, such investments would trigger problems for the collective fund under the securities laws. The SEC has stated that if IRA assets are invested in a collective fund, the fund is considered in violation of the Securities Act of 1933 and the Investment Company Act of 1940 unless the collective fund is registered with the SEC as an investment company (mutual fund) under the 1940 Act, and the shares registered as securities under the 1933 Act. For more information, banks and examiners should refer to the "Collective Investment Funds" booklet of the *Comptroller's Handbook.*

Certain investments could generate unrelated business taxable income (UBTI) resulting in the IRA paying income taxes at trust rates. IRA trustees and custodians are responsible for filing Form 990-T and paying UBTI from the IRA. An IRA can generate UBTI in one of two ways:

**Operation of a business:** For example, the IRA owner wants to direct his or her IRA to purchase and operate a franchise. If that franchise generates more than $1,000 per year in income, the IRA trustee or custodian would be required to file Form 990-T and pay taxes on that income.

**Debt financed income:** If an IRA uses debt to enhance its investment returns, earnings attributable to that debt are subject to the UBTI tax. For example, the IRA owner directs the IRA trustee or custodian to purchase unimproved real estate in his or her IRA, and then borrows against that real estate to make improvements to the property. In such a case, the earnings attributable to that debt would be subject to the UBTI tax.

## Prohibited Transactions

IRC 408(e)(2) states that IRAs are exempt from taxation unless there is a violation of the prohibited transaction rules in IRC 4975. These prohibited transaction rules are similar to the prohibited transaction rules of qualified retirement plans under ERISA. IRC 4975 prohibits an IRA from engaging in prohibited transactions with "disqualified persons," whose definition is similar to that of parties in interest under ERISA. These rules generally preclude the owner of an IRA and certain relatives of both the owner and his or her spouse from having any involvement with the IRA holdings other than directing investments.

Certain investments, such as real estate, are permissible but create a greater likelihood of prohibited transaction violations. For example, an IRA can own individual parcels of real estate, but the IRA owner and certain family members cannot have any involvement with the real estate. The IRA owner cannot live on it or act as the property manager. Even certain, seemingly inconsequential acts by the IRA owner, such as clearing debris off the land, may result in a prohibited transaction.

An IRA can both borrow in its individual capacity and make loans to other individuals or entities, but there are specific limitations on each. If the IRA borrows funds, the security for the loan cannot be any assets held outside the IRA, and the IRA owner or certain family members may not make any guarantees. Additionally, the IRA owner may not pledge the account as security for a personal loan. Failure to follow these rules results in a prohibited transaction.

An IRA may make loans but is subject to strict rules. An IRA may not make loans to the IRA owner or certain members of the owner's family. The IRA owner may not personally benefit in any way from the loan.

The consequences of a prohibited transaction involving an IRA are severe. The IRA is deemed to have distributed all its assets on the first day of the calendar year in which the prohibited transaction occurred.

There are two PTEs relating to financial institutions and IRAs.

PTE 93-1 (sometimes referred to as the free toaster exemption) permits individuals to receive cash, premiums, or other considerations paid by a financial institution in connection with the establishment of, or additional contributions to an IRA or a Keogh Plan (retirement plan for a self-employed individual), provided that certain conditions are met. Meeting all the conditions is important in order for individuals to avoid having their IRAs lose tax-exempt status because of a violation of the prohibited transaction provisions of IRC 4975. The conditions are

- the IRA or Keogh Plan (in connection with which cash, property, or other consideration is given) is established solely to benefit the participant, his or her spouse, and their beneficiaries.

- the cash, property, or other consideration is given only in connection with the establishment of the IRA or Keogh Plan, or the making of an additional contribution, including the transfer of assets from another plan, to an existing IRA or Keogh Plan.
- during any taxable year, the total of the fair market value of the property or other consideration to the sponsor of the IRA or Keogh Plan and the cash received is not more than: (1) $10 for deposits to the IRA or Keogh Plan of less than $5,000; and (2) $20 for deposits to the IRA or Keogh Plan of $5,000 or more.
- in any case where the consideration provided by a financial institution to an individual for whose benefit an IRA or Keogh Plan is established or maintained, is group term life insurance, the limitations above shall not apply to the provision of such insurance if, during any taxable year, no more than $5,000 of the face value of the insurance is attributable on a dollar-for-dollar basis to the assets of the IRA or Keogh Plan.

The relief provided by this exemption does not extend to IRAs that are part of an employer-sponsored plan (such as SEP-IRAs and SIMPLE IRAs.)

PTE 93-33 permits individuals to receive services at reduced or no cost from a financial institution when the deposit balances of the individual's IRA, Keogh Plan, SEP-IRA or SIMPLE IRA are taken into consideration for purposes of determining eligibility to receive banking services at reduced or no cost (relationship banking). Meeting the conditions in the PTE is important in order for individuals not to have their IRAs lose their tax-exempt status because of a violation of the prohibited transaction provisions of IRC 4975 and ERISA 406. The conditions are

- the IRA, Keogh Plan, SEP-IRA, or SIMPLE IRA, the deposit balance of which is taken into account for purposes of determining eligibility to receive services at reduced or no cost, is established and maintained for the exclusive purpose of the participant covered under the IRA, Keogh Plan, SEP, or SIMPLE IRA, or his or her spouse or their beneficiaries.
- the services must be of the type that the bank itself could offer, consistent with applicable federal and state banking law.
- the services are provided by the bank (or an affiliate of the bank) in the ordinary course of the bank's business to customers who qualify for reduced or no cost banking services, but who do not maintain an IRA, Keogh Plan, SEP, or SIMPLE IRA with the bank.
- for purposes of determining eligibility to receive services at reduced or no cost, the deposit balance required by the bank for the IRA or Keogh Plan is equal to the lowest balance required for any other type of account that the bank includes to determine eligibility to receive reduced or no cost services.
- the rate of return on the IRA, Keogh Plan, SEP, or SIMPLE IRA investment is no less favorable than the rate of return on an identical investment that could have been made at the same time at the same branch of the bank by a customer of the bank who is not eligible for (or who does not receive) reduced or no cost services.

The DOL has issued several AOs regarding IRAs. Listed below are some of the more recent AOs that may be of interest to financial institutions:

- **AO 2011-09A issued October 20, 2011:** Whether PTE 80-26 provides relief for an indemnification agreement between an IRA owner and a broker, when such agreement is required for the IRA to engage in futures trading.
- **AO 2011-04A issued February 3, 2011:** Whether a prohibited transaction under IRC 4975(c)(1) occurs if an individual causes his or her IRA to acquire a promissory note from a third-party bank where the individual and spouse are obligors on the note.
- **AO 2009-02A issued October 27, 2009:** Whether an IRA owner's granting to a broker of a security interest in assets held in his or her non-IRAs to cover potential indebtedness of an IRA established with the broker would result in prohibited transactions under IRC 4975.
- **AO 2005-10A issued May 11, 2005:** When fees received by a bank or an affiliate, in connection with investments in certain mutual funds by IRAs or other qualified retirement plans, are offset against management fees charged by the bank to the plans, would the receipt and offset avoid prohibited transactions under IRC 4975(c)(1)(E) or (F).
- **AO 2000-10A issued July 27, 2000:** Whether allowing the owner of an IRA to direct the IRA to invest in a limited partnership, in which relatives and the IRA owner in his or her individual capacity are partners, violates IRC 4975.

## Reporting and Disclosure Requirements

Form 5498, IRC 408(i), and 26 CFR 1.408-5 require the trustee or custodian of an IRA to make certain annual reports regarding the account to the Secretary of the Treasury and to the individual for whom such account is maintained. The report must contain information with respect to contributions and distributions aggregating $10 or more in any calendar year. Trustees and custodians must give individuals the report no later than January 31 of each year and to the IRS by May 31. IRS Form 5498 is the prescribed form for satisfying the annual reporting requirements of IRC 408(i). Form 5498 requires the trustee or custodian to provide a fair market value of the IRA assets as of December 31. This is a relatively easy task for traditional investments such as bank accounts and marketable securities. It becomes much more difficult when unique assets are involved, such as real estate, notes receivable, limited partnerships, and securities issued by closely held corporations.

Banks should note that the instructions for box 5 (Fair Market Value) of IRS Form 5498 contains a caution that states that "Trustees and custodians are responsible for ensuring that all IRA assets (including those not traded on established markets or with otherwise readily determinable market value) are valued annually at their fair market value."

According to an IRS interpretive letter issued to Partnership Valuations Inc., dated February 24, 1993, the trustee or custodian is responsible for determining the fair market value of the IRA assets and cannot evade valuation responsibility by having the participant sign a release, indemnification, or other waiver. There is another IRS interpretive letter issued to Mike Posey, president of the Retirement Industry Trust Association, dated August 6, 1993, which provides guidance on the reporting of limited partnership interests. For these investments, the IRS states that as long as the trustee reports the information that it receives from the general partners in a limited partnership, or if the general partners are not forthcoming with the fair market value information, the trustee is under no obligation to appraise the investment independently. The IRS goes on to state, if the information is unreasonable on its face or is not received, a trustee may want to reevaluate whether to continue in a fiduciary relationship with the partnership.

Banks and examiners who want more information should refer to the "Unique and Hard-to-Value Assets" booklet of the *Comptroller's Handbook*.

**Form 1099-R:** Under 26 CFR 1.408-7, the trustee or custodian of an IRA who makes a distribution during any calendar year to an individual from such account shall make a report on IRS form 1099-R. The report must show the name and address of the person, the aggregate amount of the distribution, and other information as required on the form. Trustees and custodians must give a copy of the form to the individual receiving the distribution by January 31, and a copy to the IRS by the end of February.

**Note:** The IRS will increase its attention on hard-to-value assets in IRA accounts through the addition of new codes for the 2014 1099-R and 5498 forms for IRA assets that do not have a readily available fair market value.

The changes are not mandatory for 2014 (http://www.irs.gov/Retirement-Plans/Reporting-for-Hard-to-Value-IRA-Investments-is-Optional-for-2014). The changes are not mandatory for 2014, according to the IRS, because financial institutions need a reasonable amount of time to fully implement the new requirements.

The instructions for both the 2014 1099 and 5498 forms are at http://www.irs.gov/pub/irs-pdf/i1099r.pdf. The instructions provide details related to the new codes.

**Statement of required minimum distribution:** Under 26 CFR 1.408-8 Q-10, trustees and custodians of an IRA are required to report information to the IRA owner with respect to the minimum amount required to be distributed from the IRA each calendar year. The IRS, in Notice 2002-27, furnished more information regarding the minimum distribution reporting requirement. In accordance with this notice, if a minimum distribution is required with respect to an IRA for a calendar year, and the IRA owner is alive at the beginning of the year, the trustee or custodian that held the IRA as of December 31 of the prior year must provide a statement to the IRA owner by January 3 of the subsequent calendar year regarding the required minimum distribution in accordance with one of two alternatives:

- **Alternative one:** An IRA trustee or custodian furnishes the IRA owner with a statement of the amount of the required minimum distribution with respect to the IRA for the calendar year and the distribution date.
- **Alternative two:** An IRA trustee or custodian provides a statement to the IRA owner that (1) informs the IRA owner that a minimum distribution, with respect to the IRA, is required for the calendar year and the date by which such amount must be distributed and

(2) includes an offer to furnish the IRA owner, upon request, with a calculation of the amount of the required minimum distribution with respect to the IRA for that calendar year. Under current IRS rules, there is no obligation to provide a required minimum distribution statement to the beneficiary of an inherited IRA.

Under both alternatives, the statement must also inform the IRA owner that the trustee or custodian will be reporting to the IRS (on Form 5498) that the IRA owner is required to receive a minimum distribution for the calendar year.

**Disclosure statement:** Under 26 CFR 1.408-6(d)(4)(ii)(A)(1), the trustee or custodian of an IRA account shall furnish a disclosure statement and a copy of the trust agreement to the IRA owner at least seven days before the earlier of the date of establishment or purchase of the IRA account. The trustee or custodian, however, does not have to give the IRA owner the disclosure statement until the date the IRA account is established or purchased, provided the IRA owner is given at least seven days from that date to revoke the IRA. The trustee or custodian may choose to provide the IRA owner with an IRS publication that contains the required disclosure information in lieu of providing a disclosure statement. If the trustee or custodian mails the disclosure statement and the copy of the trust agreement, then the regulations deems the individual to have received the information seven days after the date of mailing. The disclosure statement must explain certain items in plain language. For example, the statement should explain when and how to revoke an IRA, including the name, address, and telephone number of the person to receive the notice of cancellation. This explanation must appear at the beginning of the disclosure statement.

# Appendix C: ERISA

The primary objective of ERISA, codified at 29 USC 1001 et seq., and interpreted through regulations by the EBSA at 29 CFR Chapter XXV, is to protect the rights and interests of employee benefit plan participants and their beneficiaries. ERISA establishes standards for the administration of retirement plans and the investment of a plan's assets. ERISA consists of four major titles:

- Title I contains definitions and general rules applicable to retirement plans, as well as provisions on fiduciary responsibility, reporting and disclosure, and enforcement.
- Title II amends the original IRC provisions relating to retirement plans.
- Title III establishes interagency jurisdiction and mandates coordination and exchanges of information between supervisory agencies.
- Title IV establishes the PBGC, an insurance fund for defined benefit pension plans that is funded by annual premiums assessed against plans.

The provisions of title I are of particular interest to banks offering retirement plan services. Among title I's requirements for establishing a retirement plan is a written plan detailing the administration of the plan and the assignment of responsibilities for management and administration. Part 4 of title I establishes fiduciary responsibilities. The following pages contain selected definitions from ERISA related to retirement plans and a summary of part 4.

## Selected Definitions

Title I - Protection of Employee Benefit Rights; §3 - ERISA Definitions

For purposes of this title:

(2)(A) Except as provided in subparagraph (B), the terms "employee pension benefit plan" and "pension plan" mean any plan, fund, or program which was heretofore or is hereafter established or maintained by an employer or by an employee organization, or by both, to the extent that by its express terms or as a result of surrounding circumstances such plan, fund, or program—

i. provides retirement income to employees, or
ii. results in a deferral of income by employees for periods extending to the termination of covered employment or beyond, regardless of the method of calculating the contributions made to the plan, the method of calculating the benefits under the plan, or the method of distributing benefits from the plan. A distribution from a plan, fund, or program shall not be treated as made in a form other than retirement income or as a distribution prior to termination of covered employment solely because such distribution is made to an employee who has attained age 62 and who is not separated from employment at the time of such distribution.

(7) The term "participant" means any employee or former employee of an employer, or any member or former member of an employee organization, who is or may become eligible to

receive a benefit of any type from an employee benefit plan which covers employees of such employer or members of such organization, or whose beneficiaries may be eligible to receive any such benefit.

(8) The term "beneficiary" means a person designated by a participant, or by the terms of an employee benefit plan, who is or may become entitled to a benefit there under.

(9) The term "person" means an individual, partnership, joint venture, corporation, mutual company, joint-stock company, trust, estate, unincorporated organization, association, or employee organization.

(14) The term "party in interest" means, as to an employee benefit plan—

(A) any fiduciary (including, but not limited to, any administrator, officer, trustee, or custodian), counsel, or employee of such employee benefit plan;
(B) a person providing services to such plan;
(C) an employer any of whose employees are covered by such plan;
(D) an employee organization any of whose members are covered by such plan;
(E) an owner, direct or indirect, of 50 percent or more of—
    (i) the combined voting power of all classes of stock entitled to vote or the total value of shares of all classes of stock of a corporation,
    (ii) the capital interest or the profits interest of a partnership, or
    (iii) the beneficial interest of a trust or unincorporated enterprise, which is an employer or an employee organization described in subparagraph (C) or (D);
(F) a relative (as defined in paragraph (15)) of any individual described in subparagraph (A), (B), (C), or (E);
(G) a corporation, partnership, or trust or estate of which (or in which) 50 percent or more of—
    (i) the combined voting power of all classes of stock entitled to vote or the total value of shares of all classes of stock of such corporation,
    (ii) the capital interest or profits interest of such partnership, or
    (iii) the beneficial interest of such trust or estate, is owned directly or indirectly, or held by persons described in subparagraph (A), (B), (C), (D), or (E);
(H) an employee, officer, director (or an individual having powers or responsibilities similar to those of officers or directors), or a 10 percent or more shareholder directly or indirectly, of a person described in subparagraph (B), (C), (D), (E), or (G), or of the employee benefit plan; or
(I) a 10 percent or more (directly or indirectly in capital or profits) partner or joint venturer of a person described in subparagraph (B), (C), (D), (E), or (G).

The Secretary of Labor, after consultation and coordination with the Secretary of the Treasury, may by regulation prescribe a percentage lower than 50 percent of subparagraphs (E) and (G) and lower than 10 percent for subparagraph (H) or (I). The Secretary may prescribe regulations for determining the ownership (direct or indirect) of profits and beneficial interests, and the manner in which indirect stockholdings are taken into account. Any person who is a party in interest with respect to a plan to which a trust described in section 501(c)(22) of the IRC of 1986 is permitted to make payments under section 4223 shall be treated as a party in interest with respect to such trust.

(15) The term "relative" means a spouse, ancestor, lineal descendant, or spouse of a lineal descendant.

(16)(A) The term "administrator" means—
  (i) the person specifically so designated by the terms of the instrument under which the plan is operated;
  (ii) if an administrator is not so designated, the plan sponsor; or
  (iii) in the case of a plan for which an administrator is not designated and a plan sponsor cannot be identified, such other person as the Secretary may by regulation prescribe.
(B) The term "plan sponsor" means
  (i) the employer in the case of an employee benefit plan established or maintained by a single employer,
  (ii) the employee organization in the case of a plan established or maintained by an employee organization, or
  (iii) in the case of a plan established or maintained by two or more employers or jointly by one or more employers and one or more employee organizations, the association, committee, joint board of trustees, or other similar group of representatives of the parties who establish or maintain the plan.

(21)(A) Except as otherwise provided in subparagraph (B), a person is a fiduciary with respect to a plan to the extent
  (i) he exercises any discretionary authority or discretionary control respecting management of such plan or exercises any authority or control respecting management or disposition of its assets,
  (ii) he renders investment advice for a fee or other compensation, direct or indirect, with respect to any moneys or other property of such plan, or has any authority or responsibility to do so, or (iii) he has any discretionary authority or discretionary responsibility in the administration of such plan. Such term includes any person designated under section 405(c)(1)(B).
(B) If any money or other property of an employee benefit plan is invested in securities issued by an investment company registered under the Investment Company Act of 1940, such investment shall not by itself cause such investment company or such investment company's investment adviser or principal underwriter to be deemed to be a fiduciary or a party in interest as those terms are defined in this title, except insofar as such investment company or its investment adviser or principal underwriter acts in connection with an employee benefit plan covering employees of the investment company, the investment adviser, or its principal underwriter. Nothing contained in this subparagraph shall limit the duties imposed on such investment company, investment adviser, or principal underwriter by any other law.

(26) The term "current value" means fair market value where available and otherwise the fair value as determined in good faith by a trustee or a named fiduciary (as defined in section

402(a)(2)) pursuant to the terms of the plan and in accordance with regulations of the Secretary, assuming an orderly liquidation at the time of such determination.

(34) The term "individual account plan" or "defined contribution plan" means a pension plan which provides for an individual account for each participant and for benefits based solely upon the amount contributed to the participant's account, and any income, expenses, gains and losses, and any forfeitures of accounts of other participants which may be allocated to such participant's account.

(35) The term "defined benefit plan" means a pension plan other than an individual account plan; except that a pension plan which is not an individual account plan and which provides a benefit derived from employer contributions which is based partly on the balance of the separate account of a participant—

(A) for the purposes of section 202, shall be treated as an individual account plan, and
(B) for the purposes of paragraph (23) of this section and section 204, shall be treated as an individual account plan to the extent benefits are based upon the separate account of a participant and as a defined benefit plan with respect to the remaining portion of benefits under the plan.

(38) The term "investment manager" means any fiduciary (other than a trustee or named fiduciary, as defined in section 402(a)(2))—

(A) who has the power to manage, acquire, or dispose of any asset of a plan;
(B) who (i) is registered as an investment adviser under the Investment Advisers Act of 1940; (ii) is not registered as an investment adviser under such Act by reason of paragraph (1) of section 203A(a) of such Act, is registered as an investment adviser under the laws of the State (referred to in such paragraph (1)) in which it maintains its principal office and place of business, and, at the time the fiduciary last filed the registration form most recently filed by the fiduciary with such State in order to maintain the fiduciary's registration under the laws of such State, also filed a copy of such form with the Secretary; (iii) is a bank, as defined in that Act; or (iv) is an insurance company qualified to perform services described in subparagraph (A) under the laws of more than one State; and
(C) has acknowledged in writing that he is a fiduciary with respect to the plan.

## Summary of ERISA Title 1, Part 4—Fiduciary Responsibility

ERISA defines "fiduciary" in ERISA (3)(21)(a). ERISA establishes specific rules governing the conduct of all plan fiduciaries and specifies certain transactions as prohibited. Outlined below in summary form are the major provisions of ERISA title 1, part 4, which establish fiduciary responsibilities. Examiners should review the complete provisions of ERISA when evaluating a specific fact situation.

## ERISA 401—Coverage

Not every employee benefit plan is subject to ERISA's fiduciary responsibility rules. Specifically exempted are governmental plans, church plans, plans maintained outside the United States for the benefit of nonresident aliens, and nonqualified employee pension benefit plans.

## ERISA 402—Establishment of Plan

Every employee benefit plan must be established in accordance with a written plan. Such plans must provide for one or more named fiduciaries that jointly or severally have authority to control and manage the operation and administration of the plan. Every plan must

- specify a procedure for carrying out the funding policy of the plan.
- delegate to named fiduciaries responsibility for the operation and administration of the plan.
- specify the basis for contributions to and payments from the plan.
- provide a procedure for amending the plan.

Plan sponsors are generally responsible for ensuring that a plan meets the requirements of ERISA.

## ERISA 403—Establishment of Trust

ERISA 403(a) provides that all assets of an employee benefit plan shall be held in trust by one or more trustees. The trustee(s) shall be either named in the trust instrument or plan document, or appointed by a named fiduciary. The trustee(s) shall have the exclusive authority and discretion to manage and control the assets of the plan, except to the extent that

- the plan expressly provides that the trustee(s) are subject to the direction of a named fiduciary. In this case, the trustee(s) shall act in accordance with proper directions of such fiduciary. Proper directions are made in accordance with the terms of the plan and ERISA.
- authority to manage assets of the plan is delegated to one or more investment managers.

ERISA 403(b) provides certain exemptions from the rule that assets be held in trust. For example, assets of a plan that consist of insurance contracts or policies, or other assets held by an insurance company, are excluded.

ERISA 403(c) contains the requirement that the assets of the plan shall never inure to the benefit of any employer and shall be held for the exclusive purposes of providing benefits to participants and their beneficiaries and defraying reasonable expenses of administering the plan.

## ERISA 404—Fiduciary Duties

ERISA 404 outlines four fiduciary standards of care that are discussed within the body of this booklet:

- The exclusive purpose rule
- The prudent man rule
- Diversification
- Compliance with plan documents

ERISA 404(c) addresses fiduciary liability with regards to individual account plans where participants exercise control over the assets in their accounts. While the participants are not deemed to be fiduciaries, if the requirements of ERISA 404(c) are met, other fiduciaries shall not be liable for losses resulting from the participant's exercise of control. ERISA 404(c) is also discussed elsewhere in this booklet.

## ERISA 405—Liability for Breach by Co-Fiduciary

A retirement plan fiduciary may be subject to liability from the acts of another fiduciary. This liability may occur even when the fiduciary is acting in directed or nondiscretionary capacity. Private pension plan fiduciaries are liable under ERISA 405 for a breach of fiduciary responsibility committed by another fiduciary, with respect to the same plan in the following circumstances:

- If the fiduciary knowingly participates in, or undertakes to conceal, an act or omission of another fiduciary, knowing such an act or omission is a breach;
- If, by his or her failure to comply with ERISA 404(a)(1) in the administration of his or her specific responsibilities which give rise to his or her status as a fiduciary, he or she has enabled such other fiduciary to commit a breach; or
- If he or she has knowledge of a breach by such other fiduciary, unless he or she makes reasonable efforts to remedy the breach.

## ERISA 406—Prohibited Transactions

ERISA 406(a) prohibits a fiduciary from knowingly causing a plan to engage in transactions with parties in interest that constitute a direct or indirect

- sale, exchange, or leasing of any property.
- lending of money or other extension of credit.
- furnishing of goods, services, or facilities.
- transferring of plan assets to a party in interest, or use of plan assets by (or for the benefit of) a party in interest.
- acquiring of plan sponsor's securities or real property. (Special exemptions are included in ERISA 407.)

ERISA 406(b) prohibits self-dealing by plan fiduciaries:

- Dealing with a plan's assets in his or her own interest or for his or her own benefit.
- Acting on behalf of a party whose interests are adverse to the interests of the plan, its participants or beneficiaries, in any transaction involving the plan.
- Receiving any consideration for himself or herself from any party dealing with the plan in connection with a transaction involving assets of the plan.

## ERISA 407—10 Percent Limitation With Respect to Acquisition and Holding of Employer Securities and Employer Real Property by Certain Plans

This section allows a plan to acquire or hold QES or QERP under certain circumstances. The general rule, which applies to defined benefit plans, is that a plan may not acquire QES or QERP if, immediately after such acquisition, the aggregate, fair market value of employer securities and employer real property held by the plan exceeds 10 percent of the fair market value of total plan assets. This rule does not apply to eligible individual account plans (i.e., defined contribution plans). ESOPs are exempt from the 10 percent limitation and are subject to specific ESOP rules.

ERISA 407(d)(4) and (5) define QES and QERP. There are a number of restrictions on QERP, including the requirement that the real property consist of a substantial number of parcels that are geographically dispersed.

Title I—Part 4 - ERISA § 407(d)(4) and (d)(5) Definitions of QES and QERP

(4) The term "qualifying employer real property" means parcels of employer real property—
    (A) if a substantial number of the parcels are dispersed geographically;
    (B) if each parcel of real property and the improvements thereon are suitable (or adaptable without excessive cost) for more than one use;
    (C) even if all of such real property is leased to one lessee (which may be an employer, or an affiliate of an employer); and
    (D) if the acquisition and retention of such property comply with the provisions of this part (other than section 404(a)(1)(B) to the extent it requires diversification, and sections 404(a)(1)(C), 406, and subsection (a) of this section).

(5) The term "qualifying employer security" means an employer security which is—
    (A) stock,
    (B) a marketable obligation (as defined in subsection (e)), or
    (C) an interest in a publicly traded partnership (as defined in section 7704(b) of the Internal Revenue Code of 1986), but only if such partnership is an existing partnership as defined in section 10211(c)(2)(A) of the Revenue Act of 1987 (Public Law 100-203).

## ERISA 408—Exemptions From Prohibited Transactions

ERISA 408 contains statutory exemptions and provides for the Secretary of Labor to establish a procedure pursuant to which exemptions from the prohibited transaction rules may be granted. Statutory exemptions include the following:

- Loans to ESOPs
- Loans to participants
- Investment in bank deposits
- Use of bank collective investment funds
- Investment advice provided under an eligible investment advice arrangement
- Offering ancillary services

For more information, refer to appendix D, "Prohibited Transactions," of this booklet.

## ERISA 409—Liability for Breach of Fiduciary Duty

Any fiduciary that breaches any of the responsibilities, obligations, or duties imposed upon fiduciaries by title 4 shall be personally liable to make good to such plan any losses resulting from the breach. The fiduciary must also restore to such plan any profits the fiduciary gained through use of plan assets. The fiduciary shall also be subject to such other equitable or remedial relief as the court may deem appropriate, including removal of such fiduciary. No fiduciary shall be liable for a breach of fiduciary duty that was committed before he or she became a fiduciary or after he or she ceased to be a fiduciary.

## ERISA 410—Exculpatory Provisions; Insurance

Generally, any provision in an agreement or instrument which purports to relieve a fiduciary from responsibility or liability for any responsibility, obligation, or duty under this part shall be void as against public policy. This does not preclude a fiduciary from purchasing insurance to cover liability for his or her actions, or a plan or employer from purchasing insurance for its fiduciaries, or for itself to cover liability or losses occurring by reason of an act or omission of a fiduciary (with certain conditions).

## ERISA 411—Prohibition Against Certain Persons Holding Certain Positions

Section 411 prohibits a person convicted of certain crimes, such as embezzlement, bribery, or extortion, from serving in any capacity with regard to an employee benefit plan for a period of time after such conviction or the end of their imprisonment. The prohibition applies to both the individual and the hiring party. Penalties include fines up to $10,000, imprisonment for not more than five years, or both.

## ERISA 412—Bonding

In general, each fiduciary or other person who handles the assets of a plan must be bonded. Corporate fiduciaries with capital of at least $1,000,000 are exempt. For nonexempt parties, the amount of bond is 10 percent of the assets handled, with a minimum of $1,000 and a maximum of $500,000.

# Appendix D: Prohibited Transactions

The prohibited transaction rules bar parties in interest, including fiduciaries, from engaging in certain transactions. A fiduciary that engages in a prohibited transaction has breached its fiduciary responsibility, which may lead to personal liability for losses to the plan. In addition, a person who participates in a prohibited transaction is subject to a 15 percent excise tax on the amount involved. An excise tax of 100 percent may be added if the prohibited transaction is not promptly corrected.

Exemptions from the prohibited transaction rules are available. A number of exemptions are statutory. A number of individual exemptions from the prohibited transaction rules have been granted. Class exemptions are also available. Unlike individual exemptions, which offer relief only to the specific parties requesting an exemption, class exemptions furnish relief to any parties who engage in transactions of the type covered by the class exemption, if the parties meet stated terms and conditions.

All qualified plans, as well as qualified annuity plans, bond purchase plans, and IRAs, are subject to the prohibited transaction rules. Excluded from the prohibited transaction rules are governmental plans and church plans that have not elected to be subject to the participation, vesting, and funding rules of ERISA.

Prohibited transaction rules are included in ERISA and in the IRC. ERISA prohibitions affect "parties in interest" and the IRC prohibitions affect "disqualified persons." The two terms are substantially the same in most respects, but the ERISA terms include a somewhat broader range of persons. Another difference is that under ERISA provisions, for certain prohibited transactions, a fiduciary is liable only if the fiduciary knew or should have known that he or she engaged in a prohibited transaction. The IRC has not incorporated this knowledge requirement.

Under ERISA's Reorganization plan of 1978, general authority of the Secretary of the Treasury to issue regulations, rulings, opinions, and exceptions under IRC 4975 concerning tax on prohibited transactions was transferred to the Secretary of Labor. The Secretary of the Treasury retains the authority to determine and collect excise taxes.

It is important to remember that 12 CFR 9 for national banks and 12 CFR 150 for federal savings associations and other applicable laws governing conflicts of interest and self-dealing apply for all retirement plans (even nonqualified plans, which are not subject to ERISA's fiduciary and prohibited transaction rules.)

ERISA 406 addresses prohibited transactions in two parts. The first part, 406(a) prohibits fiduciaries of plans from causing the plan to engage in transactions with parties in interest. The second part, 406(b), prohibits transactions that may involve self-dealing or other fiduciary misconduct.

## ERISA Prohibited Transactions

ERISA 406(a) prohibits a fiduciary from knowingly causing an ERISA-governed plan to engage in five types of transactions between the plan and parties in interest. These prohibited transactions constitute a direct or indirect

- sale, exchange, or lease of any property.
- loan (including any extension of credit).
- provision of goods, services, or facilities.
- transfer of plan assets to a party in interest (or use of plan assets by or for the benefit of a party in interest).
- acquisition of plan sponsor's securities or real property. (Special exemptions are included in ERISA 407.)

ERISA 406(b) prohibits a fiduciary from

- dealing with a plan's assets in its own interest or for its own benefit.
- acting on behalf of a party whose interests are adverse to the interests of the plan, its participants, or beneficiaries in any transaction involving the plan.
- receiving any consideration for itself from any party dealing with the plan in connection with a transaction involving assets of the plan.

## Prohibited Transaction Exemptions

While the prohibitions of ERISA 406 are extensive, and the penalties can be severe (engaging in a prohibited transaction is a breach of fiduciary responsibility, and the IRS may assess an excise tax of up to 100 percent of the amount involved), there are numerous exemptions to the prohibited transaction restrictions.

## ERISA 407—10 Percent Limitation With Respect to Acquisition and Holding of Employer Securities and Employer Real Property by Certain Plans

ERISA 407 was intended to address Congress's concern that a number of employee benefit plans incurred major losses because they had placed large amounts of assets in employer securities or employer real property. Under ERISA 407, plans may not acquire or hold employer securities or employer real property unless they are "qualifying employer securities" or "qualifying employer real property."

Additionally, plans may not acquire employer securities or employer real property if, immediately after the acquisition, the aggregate fair market value of the investment exceeds a statutory limit of 10 percent of the fair market value of all the assets of the plan. The 10 percent limitation of ERISA 407 does not apply to "eligible individual account plans," which include most 401(k) plans and profit-sharing plans (see ERISA 407(b)(1)).

Under DOL regulations at 29 CFR 2550.407a-2, "acquisitions" of employer securities and employer real property that are subject to the 10 percent limitation include acquisition by purchase, exchange of plan assets, exercise of warrants or rights, by the conversion of a security, by default of a loan where the qualifying employer security or qualifying employer real property was security for the loan, or by the contribution of such securities or real property to the plan. Not counted towards the 10 percent limitation are acquisitions of securities as a result of a stock dividend or stock split. In addition, any acquisition or sale of employer securities or employer real property between a plan and a party in interest must meet the conditions of ERISA 408(e), which provides that the acquisition, sale, or lease be for adequate consideration and that no commission be charged (see also 29 CFR 2550.408e).

An acquisition of employer securities or employer real property that does not meet the requirements of ERISA 407 is a prohibited transaction in violation of ERISA 406(a)(1)(E) and 406(a)(2).

## ERISA 408—Statutory Exemptions

### Plan Loan Statutory Exemption—408(b)(1)

Loans are exempt from the prohibited transaction rules if made by the plan to parties in interest who are participants or beneficiaries of the plan, and if such loans

- are made in accordance with specific plan provisions.
- are available to all participants on a reasonably equivalent basis.
- are not made available to highly compensated employees in an amount greater than the amount made available to other employees.
- have a reasonable rate of return.
- are adequately secured.

DOL regulations (29 CFR 2550.408b-1) further explain each condition of the exemption. The tax treatment of participant loans made from qualified employer plans to plan participants is contained in the IRC 72(p).

### Necessary Services—408(b)(2)

ERISA 408(b)(2) permits a plan to receive office space, legal, accounting, or other services from a party in interest. The office space or service must be necessary for the establishment or operations of the plan and be under a contract or arrangement that is reasonable. And, finally, the plan may pay only reasonable compensation. DOL regulations at 29 CFR 2550.408b-2 contain definitions for all of these terms. It is important to note that this statutory exemption only provides relief from the prohibitions of ERISA 406(a) and not from ERISA 406(b).

## ESOP—Loans to Plans 408(b)(3)

Leveraged ESOPs are common. In leveraged ESOPS, the financing of the purchase of employer securities is through loans guaranteed by one or more parties in interest. The guarantee of the loan by a party in interest is a prohibited transaction. ERISA 408(b)(3) (IRC 4975(d)(3)) provides an exemption, however, from the prohibited transaction provisions of ERISA 406(a), 406(b)(1) and 406(b)(2) for loans to an ESOP that are guaranteed by a party in interest (29 CFR 2550.408b-3).

The exemption requires the loan to the plan to be

- primarily for the benefit of participants and beneficiaries of the plan (29 CFR 2550.408b-3(c)).
- at a reasonable interest rate (29 CFR 2550.408b-3(g)).

A loan that is exempt under 408(b)(3) must be nonrecourse against the plan and the plan may give as collateral only qualifying employer securities (as defined under 407) that were acquired with the exempt loan or that were used as collateral on a prior exempt loan repaid with the proceeds of the current exempt loan.

## Bank Deposits—408(b)(4)

When the bank is a fiduciary or other party in interest to a plan, ERISA 408(b)(4) provides a statutory exemption that permits plan assets to be invested in the bank's own deposits. This exemption provides relief from ERISA 406(a) as well as 406(b)(1) and (b)(2), but not (b)(3). The deposit account must generate a reasonable interest rate. The plans permitted to be invested in these deposit accounts are plans covering only employees of the bank or its affiliates, and plans that expressly permit such investments (either by a provision of the plan document or trust instrument, or by an authorization from plan fiduciary other than the bank who has such authority under the plan, and who directs the bank trustee to make these deposits). The DOL has issued regulations implementing this statutory exemption at 29 CFR 2550.408b-4.

## Ancillary Services—408(b)(6)

ERISA 408(b)(6) permits financial institutions to receive reasonable compensation for the provision of ancillary services, provided the institution has adopted internal safeguards to ensure the provision of such services is consistent with sound banking and financial practices, and specific guidelines are adopted on the extent to which the services are provided. This exemption provides relief from ERISA 406(a) as well as 406(b)(1) and (b)(2), but not (b)(3). There are regulations for this statutory exemption at 29 CFR 2550.408b-6.

## Collective Investment Fund—408(b)(8)

ERISA 408(b)(8) (see also IRC 4975(d)(8)) permits a transaction between a plan and a bank's collective investment fund if the transaction is a sale or purchase of an interest in the fund, the bank receives no more than reasonable compensation, and the transaction is specifically authorized by the plan, a trust agreement, or a fiduciary (other than the bank) that has the authority to manage and control plan assets.

For additional information, see the "Collective Investment Funds" booklet of the *Comptroller's Handbook*.

### Investment Advice—408(b)(14)

ERISA 408(b)(14) and its corresponding regulations at 29 CFR 2550.408g-1, provide an exemption for the provision of investment advice by fiduciaries to plan participants as long as the advice is through an "eligible investment advice arrangement." An "eligible investment advice arrangement" is an arrangement that meets certain threshold requirements, such as audit, notice, and disclosure, and either: (a) provides that any fees (including any commission or other compensation) received by the fiduciary adviser for investment advice or with respect to the investment of plan assets do not vary depending on the basis of any investment option selected; or (b) uses a computer model under an investment advice program that meets certain specified conditions in connection with the provision of investment advice to a participant or beneficiary. For more information, see the discussion of investment advice under ERISA compliance issues in this booklet's narrative section.

### Foreign Exchange Transactions—408(b)(18)

ERISA 408(b)(18), provides a prohibited transaction exemption for any foreign exchange transactions between a party in interest, bank or broker-dealer (or affiliate of either), and a plan if certain conditions are met. These conditions are

- the transaction is in connection with the purchase, holding, or sale of securities or other investment assets.
- at the time the foreign exchange transaction is entered into, the terms of the transaction are not less favorable to the plan than the terms generally available in comparable, arm's-length transactions between unrelated parties.
- the exchange rate used by the bank or broker-dealer (or affiliate) for a particular foreign exchange transaction does not deviate by more than 3 percent from the interbank bid and asked rates for transactions of comparable size and maturity at the time of the transactions displayed on an independent service that reports rates of exchange in the foreign currency market for such currency.
- the bank or broker-dealer (or any affiliate of either) does not have investment discretion, or provide investment advice, with respect to the transaction.

### Cross-Trades—408(b)(19)

The PPA of 2006 added ERISA 408(b)(19) that contains an exemption for an investment manager to cross-trade securities between ERISA accounts and other accounts managed by the same manager if certain conditions are satisfied. See a summary of these conditions in the discussion of cross-trades under Investment Management in this booklet's narrative section.

## Prohibited Transaction Class Exemptions

**Proprietary Mutual Funds—PTE 77-4**

The bank's use of investment discretion to invest retirement plan assets in the shares of affiliated investment companies (e.g., mutual funds) constitutes a prohibited transaction. PTE 77-4 covers the purchase or sale by a plan of shares of a mutual fund when the investment adviser of the mutual fund is also a fiduciary (or an affiliate thereof) with respect to the plan, and is not an employer of any of the employees covered by the plan. PTE 77-4 provides relief from the prohibitions of ERISA 406(a) and 406(b).

PTE 77-4 contains various disclosure and approval requirements. Specifically, an independent plan fiduciary must approve the investment in writing, after receiving the following information:

- A current prospectus of the mutual fund.
- A full and detailed written disclosure of the investment advisory fee and other fees charged to or paid by the plan, and the mutual fund including the nature and extent of any differential between the rates of such fees, the reasons why the fiduciary adviser considers investment in the mutual fund to be appropriate, whether there are any restrictions on which plan assets may be invested in the affiliated mutual funds and, if so, the nature of such restrictions.
- New disclosures are required if there is any change in any of the rates of fees. The independent fiduciary must approve in writing the continued purchase, sale, and holding of the mutual fund shares or be allowed to terminate the current arrangement.

A plan is prohibited from paying the bank a sales commission in connection with purchases or sales of mutual fund shares covered by the exemption. The plan also may not pay the bank fiduciary or its affiliates "double" investment advisory or investment management fees with respect to plan assets invested in the mutual fund shares. To ensure there are no violations of this "double-dipping" provision, the plan either must not pay a plan level investment advisory or management fee with respect to those assets, or must receive a credit against its plan level fee for its pro rata share of investment advisory fees paid by the mutual fund.

**Brokers Executing Securities Transactions—PTE 86-128**

PTE 86-128 provides an exemption from ERISA 406(b) violations for plan fiduciaries effecting or executing securities transactions on behalf of a plan. Expressly excluded from relief are transactions that are excessive either in amount or frequency, to prevent "churning" of plan portfolios. Extended relief for discretionary trustees, or their affiliates, was provided under this exemption in an amendment adopted in 2002. Discretionary trustees (or their affiliates) may only engage in covered transactions with a plan that has total net assets with a value of at least $50 million. In the case of a pooled fund, the $50 million requirement is met if 50 percent or more of the units of beneficial interest in the pooled fund are held by plans having total net assets with a value of at least $50 million. For purposes of the net asset tests, where a single employer or controlled group of employers maintains a group of plans, the

$50 million net asset requirement is met by aggregating the assets of such plans, if the assets are pooled for investment purposes in a single master trust. A fiduciary that is a plan administrator under ERISA or the plan sponsor does not receive relief under the PTE.

Discretionary trustees also have additional disclosure requirements under the PTE. The discretionary trustee must furnish, at least annually, to the authorizing fiduciary of the plan the following information:

- Aggregate brokerage commissions, expressed in dollars, paid by the plan to brokerage firms affiliated with the trustee.
- Aggregate brokerage commissions, expressed in dollars, paid by the plan to brokerage firms unaffiliated with the trustee.
- Average brokerage commissions, expressed as cents per share, paid by the plan to brokerage firms affiliated with the trustee.
- Average brokerage commissions, expressed as cents per share, paid by the plan to brokerage firms unaffiliated with the trustee.

There are other conditions built into the exemption to protect the interests of plan participants and beneficiaries. One of the conditions is that the authorizing fiduciary receives, on an annual basis, the following:

- The total of all securities transaction-related charges incurred by the plan.
- The amount of the securities transaction-related charges retained by the fiduciary executing securities transactions under the exemption, and the amount of these charges paid to other persons for execution or other services.
- A description of the fiduciary's brokerage placement practices, if such practices have materially changed.
- A portfolio turnover ratio, calculated in a manner reasonably designed to provide the authorizing fiduciary with the information needed to assist in discharging its duty of prudence.

### Securities Lending—PTE 2006-16

The lending of securities from employee benefit plans is a fairly common practice. When the lending is fully collateralized and the collateral is invested in a fully liquid investment, there is little risk and the plan earns additional income from the lending of the securities. Generally, securities lending takes place with a financial institution that is acting as a trustee or investment manager for the plan, as well as a securities broker or its affiliate that is providing services to the plan. In such cases, a prohibited transaction in violation of ERISA 406(a) exists because the financial institution or securities broker, or the affiliate of either, are parties in interest with respect to the plan.

PTE 2006-16 amended and replaced previously issued class exemptions that permitted securities lending (PTE 81-6 and PTE 82-63.) The new PTE incorporated PTEs 81-6 and

82-63 into one renumbered exemption and expanded the prohibited transaction relief from ERISA 406(a) and 406(b)(1) violations provided in PTEs 81-6 and 82-63 to include additional parties and additional forms of collateral subject to the many conditions stated in PTE 2006-16.

# Appendix E: Abbreviations

| | |
|---|---|
| ADP/ADC | Actual Deferral Percentage/Actual Contribution Percentage |
| AO | Advisory Opinion |
| BSA/AML | Bank Secrecy Act/Anti-Money Laundering |
| CFR | Code of Federal Regulations |
| CM | clearing member |
| CSP | covered service provider |
| DCO | designated clearing organization |
| DOL | Department of Labor |
| EACA | eligible automatic contribution arrangement |
| EBSA | Employee Benefits Security Administration |
| ERISA | Employee Retirement Income Security Act of 1974 |
| ESOP | employee stock ownership plan |
| FAB | Field Assistance Bulletin |
| FCM | futures commission merchant |
| FFIEC | Federal Financial Institutions Examination Council |
| GLBA | Gramm–Leach–Bliley Act |
| IB | Interpretive Bulletin |
| IRA | individual retirement account |
| IRC | Internal Revenue Code |
| IRS | Internal Revenue Service |
| MPPP | money purchase pension plan |
| MSP | major swap participant |

| | |
|---|---|
| OFAC | Office of Foreign Assets Control |
| PBGC | Pension Benefit Guarantee Corporation |
| PTE | prohibited transaction exemption |
| QACA | qualified automatic contribution arrangement |
| QDIA | Qualified Default Investment Alternative |
| QDRO | qualified domestic relations order |
| QERP | qualifying employer real property |
| QES | qualifying employer securities |
| RFP | request for proposal |
| SCRA | Servicemembers Civil Relief Act |
| SD | swap dealer |
| SEC | Securities and Exchange Commission |
| SEP | simplified employee pension plans |
| SIMPLE | savings incentive match plan for employees |
| TPA | third-party administrator |
| UBTI | unrelated business taxable income |
| UITRS | Uniform Interagency Trust Rating System |

# References

## Laws

Employee Retirement Income Security Act of 1974

Internal Revenue Code

26 USC 408, "Individual Retirement Accounts"

26 USC 4975, "Tax on Prohibited Transactions"

Investment Company Act of 1940

Pension Protection Act of 2006

Securities Exchange Act of 1934

Gramm–Leach–Bliley Act

Dodd–Frank Wall Street Reform and Consumer Protection Act of 2010

Commodity Exchange Act

Self-Employed Individuals Tax Retirement Act of 1962

Securities Act of 1933

## Regulations

12 CFR 9, "Fiduciary Activities of National Banks"; 12 CFR 150, "Fiduciary Powers of Federal Savings Associations"

12 CFR 12, "Recordkeeping and Confirmation Requirements for Securities Transactions" (national banks)

12 CFR 151, "Recordkeeping and Confirmation Requirements for Securities Transactions" (federal savings associations)

12 CFR 218 and 17 CFR 247, "Regulation R"

12 CFR 226.3(g), "Truth in Lending, Regulation Z"

17 CFR 23.400, "Business Conduct Standards for Swap Dealers & Major Swap Participants Dealing with Counterparties, Including Special Entities"

29 CFR Chapter XXV, "Employee Benefit Security Administration"

29 CFR 2550, "Rules and Regulations for Fiduciary Responsibility"

## Comptroller's Handbooks

### Examination Process

"Bank Supervision Process"

"Community Bank Supervision"

"Federal Branches and Agencies Supervision"

"Large Bank Supervision"

### Asset Management

"Asset Management"

"Collective Investment Funds"

"Conflicts of Interest"

"Custody Services"

"Investment Management Services"
"Personal Fiduciary Services"
"Unique and Hard-to-Value Assets"

## OCC Issuances

OCC Bulletin 2004-20, "Risk Management of New, Expanded, or Modified Bank Products and Services: Risk Management Process" (May 10, 2004)

OCC Bulletin 2006-24, "Interagency Agreement on ERISA Referrals: Information Sharing Between the FFIEC Agencies and the DOL" (June 1, 2006)

OCC Bulletin 2007-7, "Soft Dollar Guidance: Use of Commission Payments by Fiduciaries" (February 5, 2007)

OCC Bulletin 2008-10, "Fiduciary Activities of National Banks: Annual Reviews of Fiduciary Accounts Pursuant to 12 CFR 9.6(c)" (March 27, 2008)

OCC Bulletin 2010-24, "Incentive Compensation: Interagency Guidance on Sound Incentive Compensation Policies" (June 30, 2010)

OCC Bulletin 2013-29, "Third Party Relationships: Risk Management Guidance (October 30, 2013)

OCC Trust Interpretive Letter No. 40, August 1, 1986, to Robert Plotkin

## Other

**DOL**—can be accessed through EBSA Web site at www.dol.gov/ebsa/

### Advisory Opinions

79-49, Fee on Own Bank Plan
82-49A, Futures Transactions
88-02A, Sweep Services
92-23A, Purchases of Bank Holding Company Stock
92-24A, Bank Agents and Trustees, Earning Interest from "Float"
93-12A, PTE 77-4
93-13A, PTE 77-4
93-24A, Float
93-26A, Application of PTE 77-4 to IRAs
94-41A, Escheat Law Preemption
97-15A, Payment of Fees from a Mutual Fund when Bank has Discretion (Frost Letter)
97-16A, Receipt of Fees from Unrelated Mutual Funds (Aetna Letter)
97-19A, Revenue Sharing Fees paying Direct Expenses
2000-10A, Limited Partnerships, IRAs
2001-01A, Settlor & Fiduciary Plan Expenses
2001-09A, Sun America on investment advice
2001-9, Asset Allocation Services
2001-10A, Ancillary Services
2002-08A, Indemnification and Hold-harmless Provisions

2003-02A, Overdraft Protection Services

2003-09A, Receipt of Fees from Proprietary Mutual Funds

2005-10A, Offset of Fees Received in Connection with Mutual Funds

2009-02A, Security Interest, IRAs

2011-04A, Promissory Note, IRAs

2011-09A, PTE 80-26, IRAs

2013-01A, Cleared Swap Transactions

2013-03A, Revenue Sharing Payments are Plan Assets

## Prohibited Transaction Class Exemptions

PTE 77-3, Purchase or Sale of Shares of Open-End Investment Companies (Proprietary Mutual Funds)

PTE 77-4, Purchase or Sale of Shares of Open-End Investment Companies (Mutual Funds)

PTE 80-26, Interest-free Loans (Overdrafts)

PTE 81-6 (amended), Securities Lending

PTE 81-8, Short Term Investments

PTE 82-63, Securities Lending Services: Payment of Compensation

PTE 84-14, Qualified Professional Asset Manager (QPAM)

PTE 86-128 (rev.), Agency Transactions Executed by Fiduciary Broker-Dealers

PTE 93-1, Certain Transactions Involving IRAs and Plans for Self-Employed Individuals

PTE 93-33, Receipt of Certain Services in Connection with IRAs and Plans for Self-Employed Individuals

PTE 2002-12, Cross-Trades of Securities

## DOL Field Assistance Bulletins

2002-03, Disclosure and Other Obligations Relating to "Float"

2003-3, Allocation of Expenses in a Defined Contribution Plan

2004-02, Fiduciary Duties and Missing Participants in Defined Contribution Plans

2004-03, Fiduciary Responsibilities of Directed Trustees

2007-01, Statutory Exemption for Investment Advice

2008-01, Fiduciary Responsibility for Collection of Delinquent Contribution

2012-02R, Fee Disclosure Guidance for 404a-5

2013-02, Required Annual Fee Disclosure for 404a-5

## DOL Interpretive Bulletins

2509.08-2, Interpretive bulletin relating to the exercise of shareholder rights and written statements of investment policy, including proxy voting policies or guidelines

2509.75-4, Interpretive bulletin relating to indemnification of fiduciaries

2509.96-1, Interpretive bulletin relating to participant investment education

### DOL Information Letter

August 1, 1986, to Robert Plotkin
March 21, 1996, to Eugene Ludwig
August 20, 2002, to American Bankers Association

### DOL Other

"Target Date Retirement Funds—Tips for ERISA Plan Fiduciaries" (February 2013)
Technical Release No. 86-1 (May 22, 1986)—soft dollars
DOL announcement (February 4, 2013), settlement agreement with ING Life
    Insurance and Annuity Co. regarding ING's practice of keeping investment gains
    resulting from the correction of trading errors
Form 5500, Annual Return/Report of Employee Benefit Plan
Automatic Enrollment 401(k) Plans for Small Businesses

## Federal Financial Institutions Examination Council

### FFIEC Information Technology Examination Handbook
"Business Continuity Planning"
"Outsourcing Technology Services"

FFIEC Bank Secrecy Act/Anti-Money Laundering Examination Manual
FFIEC 031 and 041, Consolidated Reports of Condition and Income (call report),
    Schedule RC-T

## Internal Revenue Service

Form 5305, Traditional Individual Retirement Trust Account
Form 5305-A, Traditional Individual Retirement Custodial Account
Form 990-T, Exempt Organization Business Income Tax Return
IRS interpretive letter to Partnership Valuations Inc. (February 24, 1993)
IRS interpretive letter to Mike Posey, President of the Retirement Industry Trust
    Association (August 6, 1993)
IRS Form 1099-R
IRS Form 5498
IRS Notice 2002-27
IRS Notice 2009-68
IRS Revenue Procedure 2012-35
Revenue Ruling 81-100, Group Trusts
Revenue Ruling 95-57, Proxy Voting ESOPs

## Financial Industry Regulatory Authority

Regulatory Notice 12-05, "Verification of Emailed Instructions to Transmit or Withdraw
    Assets from Customer Accounts (January 2012)

www.ingramcontent.com/pod-product-compliance
Lightning Source LLC
Chambersburg PA
CBHW080259290526
45790CB00005B/1869